MW01120317

SOCIAL ISSUES, JUSTICE AND STATUS

BEING WITH EDGY YOUTH

SOCIAL ISSUES, JUSTICE AND STATUS

Additional books in this series can be found on Nova's website
under the Series tab.

Additional E-books in this series can be found on Nova's website
under the E-book tab.

CHILDREN'S ISSUES, LAWS AND PROGRAMS

Additional books in this series can be found on Nova's website
under the Series tab.

Additional E-books in this series can be found on Nova's website
under the E-book tab.

SOCIAL ISSUES, JUSTICE AND STATUS

BEING WITH EDGY YOUTH

KIARAS GHARABAGHI

Nova Science Publishers, Inc.

New York

Copyright © 2012 by Nova Science Publishers, Inc.

For permission to use material from this book please contact us:
Telephone 631-231-7269; Fax 631-231-8175
Web Site: http://www.novapublishers.com

NOTICE TO THE READER

The Publisher has taken reasonable care in the preparation of this book, but makes no expressed or implied warranty of any kind and assumes no responsibility for any errors or omissions. No liability is assumed for incidental or consequential damages in connection with or arising out of information contained in this book. The Publisher shall not be liable for any special, consequential, or exemplary damages resulting, in whole or in part, from the readers" use of, or reliance upon, this material. Any parts of this book based on government reports are so indicated and copyright is claimed for those parts to the extent applicable to compilations of such works.

Independent verification should be sought for any data, advice or recommendations contained in this book. In addition, no responsibility is assumed by the publisher for any injury and/or damage to persons or property arising from any methods, products, instructions, ideas or otherwise contained in this publication.

This publication is designed to provide accurate and authoritative information with regard to the subject matter covered herein. It is sold with the clear understanding that the Publisher is not engaged in rendering legal or any other professional services. If legal or any other expert assistance is required, the services of a competent person should be sought. FROM A DECLARATION OF PARTICIPANTS JOINTLY ADOPTED BY A COMMITTEE OF THE AMERICAN BAR ASSOCIATION AND A COMMITTEE OF PUBLISHERS.

Additional color graphics may be available in the e-book version of this book.

Library of Congress Cataloging-in-Publication Data

Being with edgy youth / editor, Kiaras Gharabaghi.
    p. cm.
  Includes index.
  ISBN 978-1-62100-947-4 (hbk.)
  1. Problem youth. 2. Youth with social disabilities. I. Gharabaghi, Kiaras.
  HV1421.B44 2011
  362.74--dc23
                    2011039663

Published by Nova Science Publishers, Inc. †New York

I dedicate this book to the edgy youth I have encountered along the way, especially:

Patti B., Chrissy H., Veronica H., Adam B. & Jennifer E.

CONTENTS

PREFACE

Throughout the course of my twenty-odd year career working directly with edgy youth, I have encountered some of the most wonderful people I have ever known. Many of these wonderful people were the edgy youth themselves. Resulting from the privilege of being with these youth, my life has forever been changed for the better. I also met the most fantastic professionals during those years, including the woman with whom I have been sharing my life with for the past twelve years. Among my closet friends are quite a few who have had (and in some cases still have) long careers working with edgy youth. In many respects, I feel that my involvement with edgy youth has allowed me to develop a social circle of individuals who, like me, have never been all that comfortable with whatever has been laid out for them in life. The people whom I admire most have several traits in common that seem to cut across the categories of edgy youth and professional helper. They are all critical observers of society at large, and they are not easily swayed, one way or the other, by political arguments and economic persuasion. They all appreciate a good debate about seemingly trivial issues, and although such debates are always humor-laden, no issue or theme is ever too trivial to debate. None of them are especially good with following the rules, although all of them seem pragmatic in their responses to demands from employers, law enforcement agents and government departments.

It seems that I find the greatest comfort among people who are respectfully non-compliant, reflectively non-conformist and pragmatically flexible. Among these people, I recognize the perfect balance between ideological commitments to affect change and societal movement toward more collective responsibility and greater commitments to democracy, while also maintaining a determined approach to self-improvement, opportunism and personal growth. I have learned over the years that maintaining such a balance takes a great deal of skill. Many people simply are not skilled enough to do so. When someone does it well, however, I often find that such a person turns out to have been an edgy youth at some earlier point in time, and that person typically has maintained this edgy factor from that earlier time and transformed it into a lifestyle and value system for their life span.

My first involvement with edgy youth came when I accepted a position as a front-line youth worker in a group home in Ontario. The home provided emergency housing for up to ten teenagers who had either been abandoned by their families or who were at risk of harm at the hands of their family. I learned very quickly that it really did not matter what the reason for admission was; the youth who came to this home had all experienced a combination of abuse (emotional abuse in all cases, physical abuse in many cases and sexual abuse in some cases) and rejection (from their family as well as from community institutions such as schools, public libraries and malls, or other places where young people hang out). I also learned (but by no means understood) that young people with a lifetime of these kinds of experiences adopt two core responses: they act out behaviorally against those caring for them, whether that be their family or professional staff in a group home, and they crave the attention and love of those caring for them at the same time, whether that be their family or professional staff in a group home or, most likely, both. Indeed, one of the hardest lessons I learned was that, in spite of their absolute rejection of *being* with family, these young people loved their families regardless of what might have transpired. In spite of challenging the authority and patience of the professional staff to the limit and beyond each and every day, these young people were eager to engage the staff and be engaged by them all the time.

As the years passed, I found myself working with edgy youth (and often their families) in all kinds of different settings and contexts. I worked for years in residential treatment, offered by the children's mental health sector; I worked as a family reunification worker for several child protection agencies in Canada; I did many shifts in custody facilities for youth; and I spent weeks and weeks with children and youth in hospitals to help manage their mental health crises, their suicidal ideations and their efforts at rehabilitating from accidents, trauma or addictions. Later in my career, I managed several shelter programs for homeless youth in Toronto. I was astonished to learn, in those days, that well over half the youth living in my shelters had become homeless after spending much of their lives in the care of publically operated child protection agencies.

All of these experiences served to confirm, in my mind, what I had learned during those first few months of my very first job working with edgy youth. Edgy youth are young people with enormous potential, not just in avoiding future troubles (which seems to be the bar set by much of the service system for edgy youth), but in leading their peers and all of us to a better place of democratic engagement and everyday life. Their ability to resist oppression, to fight back against those parasitic quasi-professionals seeking to dominate their every move, and to expect nothing less than miracles from themselves is precisely the foundation required to shift us from our complacency toward poverty, war, ecological disaster and other terrible things toward a renewed commitment to be kind, to be attentive to one another and to re-commit to the fundamental principles of democracy, including a voice for everyone and a place of connection for everyone as well.

Unfortunately, my years working with edgy youth in all of these different settings confirmed something else in my mind. We are terribly ill-equipped to engage edgy youth and to foster their strengths and exceptionalities that are so wonderful, and that we desperately need. It has been my experience that in spite of a small group of people being committed to engage edgy youth (and be engaged by them), for the purpose of co-creating a future that works for everyone, there is a much larger group of professionals who are committed to impose on edgy youth (and non-conforming professionals) a regime of order, control and discipline that seeks to create compliance and conformity so that the status quo is maintained for all times to come. It is not that these professionals are evil or mal-intentioned. To the contrary, most actually believe their approaches to suppress the identity and self-expression of edgy youth are a good thing: a way of helping these poor, misguided young people get it together and join a pro-social, civic-minded and tax-paying society. These are trained (sometimes untrained) professionals who sincerely believe that they know the right answer, that they have the solutions to young people's problems, and that they are working in the name of virtue and social improvement. They are undeterred by the fact that there always seems to be a group of youth who does not respond to their approaches, who get lost in the shuffle and who eventually must be abandoned because of their lack of cooperation with the professional helpers. These young people are the price we pay to maintain order among and control over the larger group of youth who succumb to the impositions of the professionals and their organizations.

I am not dismissive of this large group of professionals, even if, in my mind, they do more harm than good. I believe that they have been blinded by the simplistic and over-scientific helping communities that search for evidence of their way being the best way. Invariably, the evidence found coincidentally maintains very large and wealthy industrial complexes, including: the pharmaceutical industries, the research institutions, the increasingly entrepreneurial class of managers and quasi-scientific disciplines that have little more to offer than their reputational glory (psychiatry might fall into this category).

In my experience, edgy youth would be just fine if they could freely associate with that smaller group of professional helpers who are genuinely interested in their relationships with them and whose approach to being with the youth is driven, first and foremost, by authenticity and a deep respect for their reflective non-compliance. The difficulty is that the power of the other group of professionals extends well into the possibilities for this smaller group and limits this group's opportunities to move further along the process of being with edgy youth. "Being with", as it turns out, is devalued and rendered inefficient by the dominance of "doing to". Where the authentic professional helper understands the importance of *being with edgy youth* as the core element of the intervention, the scientifically-informed professional, seeking to prove his or her conformity to the commands of the psychiatric/managerial establishment, will spend much of his or her time *doing something* to the edgy youth in the name of assessment, treatment, diagnosis or case management. "Being with" is rearticulated as not knowing what to do, a passive form of demonstrating incompetence. We must change young people based on the evidence that we have on how to change them; never mind that we have spent virtually no time at all contemplating whether changing edgy youth into something closer to our own self image is a good thing.

After twenty-odd years of learning about edgy youth and about the professionals and their professional systems, I have written this book to once again invoke the power of being with edgy youth. I am by no means the first or only observer, participant or scholar to suggest that being with edgy youth is, in and of itself, a far more powerful intervention than doing things to them. Indeed, there is an entire discipline (in which I teach) called Child and Youth Care Practice, founded on the belief that we must learn to be with young people, to be in relationship with young people, and to be reflective and authentic in our presence with young people. It pains me to acknowledge, however, that this discipline is marginalized among the other disciplines, within the helping professions. Psychology, Social Work, Medicine and even Nursing appear to be taken far more seriously in this context than child and youth care practice. Nonetheless, I feel no need to engage in an inter-disciplinary argument about which discipline ought to be seen as the leader, in charge, or of greatest significance. It would appear self-evident, that being with edgy youth is not a disciplinary activity, but simply really good practice, reflecting defensible ethics and having greatest chance of connecting with the youth.

This book will reflect the pragmatism and critical framework presented up to this point. I have produced what I hope is a well-organized argument that I have divided into six chapters. Starting with the second chapter, each chapter provides a detailed and often unique analysis of particularly crucial elements of being with edgy youth. In the first chapter, I introduce edgy youth in the general context of young people, and also in the context of a metaphorical representation of social worlds at the center and on the edge. In this opening chapter, my goal is to highlight the complexity of what I mean by edgy youth, and, in particular, I seek to do away with the common trend which equates behavioral issues with edginess. I close this first chapter with a lengthy discussion of the view from the edge; in other words, while we have many different views from the center into the edge already, we have not spent enough time considering how edgy youth might view those of us at the center and how this might inform their responses to us. I have titled the first chapter somewhat offensively in order to capture what, in my experience, has been the most fitting response edgy youth have collectively levied against adults seeking to impose their authority and culture upon them. It is my belief that we cannot escape the depth of rejection of our scientific methods on the part of edgy youth by pretending that their language is reflective of their behavioral problems.

In chapter two, I turn my attention more directly toward the professional helpers, and I focus on the need for helpers to "get over it"; edgy youth would not be living up to their name or their reputation if they did not challenge professional helpers to the core. In order to deserve the label "professional helper", as an indication that this work is neither charity nor volunteerism, getting over the insults and the impact on oneself is an essential first step. Chapter three continues with this theme, but focuses specifically on the issue of personalizing. Although virtually all training and academic preparation associated with working with young people provides instruction not to personalize this work, I provide a much more expansive definition of personalizing and argue that this is not as simple as merely deciding to not personalize it. At any rate, there are circumstances where a failure to personalize the work appears indicative not of professionalism, but of cold and hard emotional detachment from the experiences of edgy youth.

Chapters four and five move toward the articulation of an approach associated with being with edgy youth, focusing on the shared experiences of becoming present and staying with it. I argue that not enough emphasis is placed on either the reflection of our presence in the lives of edgy youth or their presence in our lives. Using a relational framework for understanding "being together", I provide both conceptual and practical ideas that may re-ignite our passion for being with edgy youth.

Finally, in the last chapter of the book, I highlight the reasons why being with edgy youth is critical not only as an intervention on their behalf, but also as a way of ensuring a democratic and meaningful future for all of us. This chapter serves as my final assault on all those approaches in the helping professions that seek to instill compliance and conformity. We need edgy youth to become our edgy leaders of the future. Replicating our current leaders seems like a bad idea these days.

ACKNOWLEDGMENTS

Writing a book of this nature carries the risk of being misunderstood and of causing offense to those I do not wish to offend. I am always aware of my use of strong language that at times takes friends, colleagues and readers by surprise. Then again, I trust that those who share my passion for being with edgy youth, even if they choose a different path, will appreciate this work as one of many contributions to the invigorating discussions and debates already unfolding all over the world. We are stronger for our differences, our disagreements and our battles.

In recent times, I have been influenced by new friends and colleagues, including Hans Skott-Myhre, Ben Anderson-Nathe, Grant Charles, Laura Steckley and Janet Newbury. I always find comfort amongst my colleagues in the School of Child & Youth Care at Ryerson University in Toronto. My old friends and mentors still haunt my every thought: Thom Garfat, Carol Stuart, Bill Carty, Jean Cull. While writing this book, I received care, love and nurture from my brothers Kio, Tahmo & Frank, my friends Birol and Debbie, the Muskoka River and my long drives on highway 400 in Ontario.

Each and every morning I wake to the shining beauty of my wife Patricia and the chaotic awesomeness of my three children: Siena, Jett and Alex. I can't ask for any more.

Chapter 1

F@CK YOU!

We live in a world of labels. In order to make sense of what is around us and especially of the many relationships we manage every day, we impose labels on others as a way of identifying ourselves. Sometimes we use labels that are well-intended: "citizens", "taxpayers", "successful", and "good". At other times, we use labels that are designed to create distance between ourselves and those we fear, dislike or distrust: "unproductive", "bums", "criminals", "good-for-nothings", and so on. Labels help us to maintain and also to dismantle the historical divisions in our communities and societies. Racism, sexism, homophobias, ageism, and so many other "isms" that have wrought havoc on the concepts of community, inclusiveness and non-violence all continue to exist in varying degrees in different places, all coming with their very own language built on the ruins of yesterday's labels.

This book is about one particular group of people who have been subject to far more labels than anyone can remember. Indeed, a compilation of labels applied to this group would yield several volumes all by itself. In this book, I will be talking about a sub-group of young people that much of our society wishes did not exist. I have invented my very own label for this sub-group of young people: I call them "edgy youth", and I consider this a compliment.[1]

Before I say anything else about edgy youth, I want to make some general observations about young people that will help to situate edgy youth in the spectrum of demographics. Young people include all those between the ages

---

[1] There are many other terms that are commonly used to label sub-groups of young people often seen as a burden on society, including "youth-at-risk", "delinquent youth" and "troubled youth". I don't like any of these labels because they associate a problematic quality with the lifestyles of young people who do not conform to the norm. I argue that not conforming to the norm can be a strength, even if it also exposes vulnerabilities. An excellent discussion of this topic and related themes is provided in Scott-Myhre, H. (2008).

of zero and roughly twenty-four, although we would surely be making our first mistake by creating cut-offs for what makes a person a young person. Much has been written about the process of moving through childhood, into adolescence, and on to early adulthood. Indeed, developmental theory, which focuses on the changes in mental, emotional and physical capacities as a person grows, is huge, both in impact and in volume. We have organized much of our involvement with young people based on developmental milestones, and we have, over a period of centuries, grown very comfortable with universalizing our expectations of how children ought to grow up, what they ought to be able to do at what age, and how they ought to behave along the way. We demand, for example, that all children, regardless of where they live, who they are or what they want, start school at the age of six, as if this is magically the moment when all children are exactly the same. For those young people who cannot keep up with these milestones, we have an enormous array of labels that we typically dont hesitate to impose. Some of the most fun ones include: "Mild Intellectual Retardation", "Global Developmental Impairment" and "Pervasive Developmental Disability". Even those who are able to keep up with these milestones, yet have unique ways of demonstrating their capacities, are subject to an equally enormous array of labels. They are gifted with wonderful terms, such as: "conduct disordered", "oppositional defiance disordered" or "disruptive behavior disordered". The former group more generally falls into the "developmental challenges" category, while the latter group falls into the "mental health" category. Either way, there is something "wrong", "different", "deviant", or "other" than what is prescribed by our collective wisdom about how young people ought to be.

While much of the developmental and mental health literatures are based on research and evidence, and should not be dismissed solely on the grounds of their ignorance of humanity and their oppressive tendencies with respect to "being different", the core element of growing up is not captured in either literature. Yet, it is precisely this core element of growing up that creates the greatest challenge for young people, in general, and certainly for edgy youth. For the moment, at least, I would like us to put aside everything we know about the stages of developmental growth, forget Erikson and Piaget, and ignore the burgeoning literature and research evidence produced by the brain sciences. The most important thing that changes as young people grow up, the core element of human development from infancy to childhood to adolescence and into early adulthood, is that young people become less cute as they grow.

Newborns, infants and toddlers are very cute. We love to look at them and their incredibly cute and tiny body features make us smile, even grin from ear to ear, and make us offer linguistically nonsensical utterances, worthy of the literary use of the term "idiot". At this age, young people can spit on us, vomit over our clothes, keep us up at night, throw their food around, soil their clothes and smear their feces, become violent and pull our hair, and smack us on the nose or throw things at us. We delight in their cuteness, their innocence and the magic of their existence. Indeed, on their very first birthday, we throw elaborately-themed parties in their honor, for no other reason than to capture their cuteness, in spite of their complete lack of understanding of the occasion. We spend money, we fuss, we take millions of pictures that all look exactly the same: a bewildered looking baby who eats, farts and poops from morning to night. How cute.

As toddlers become preschoolers and eventually start school and become little people in their own right, their cuteness changes but remains on very solid footing. The kids learn to talk and say funny things, they wear mini-versions of our own clothes and they make it easy to reflect our own fantasy of being cute ourselves. They start to make friends and become social, and watching them find their place among their peers is inherently cute. Of course, they also become more demanding, they discover the thrill of temper tantrums, they eventually learn to say, "No", they become selective about what they want to eat, and all kinds of other things happen that are considerably less cute. But their overall being, their presence in our lives, is still governed by a high cuteness factor. Thus, our tolerance for their misdeeds and misbehaviors is also still fairly high. At any rate, even if we become really annoyed by the kids, they are still young enough to have hope for a better future. "Sure, my kid drives me crazy, but he will eventually be a hockey pro, or a rocket scientist or a famous artist" (just look at the nuanced art behind these scribbles).

As the kids get a little older still, things do start to change. Perhaps the most important change is not so much that kids aren't cute anymore, but rather that *other people's kids* are cute, so long as we don't have to be responsible for them. The concept of kids is still associated with cuteness, but parenting kids a little less so. In fact, it starts to be work and those cute little kids from yesterday suddenly have a mind of their own. They begin to challenge our previously uncontested status as household emperors. Their misdeeds are no longer symptoms of cuteness and innocence; now we call these "trouble". There are just so many places where kids can get into trouble, none as predictable, yet annoying, as school. Trouble at school means awkward moments for parents having to deal with seemingly judgmental teachers and school administrators. These are the early signs of the demise of the cuteness factor. It turns out that people who work at schools, in any capacity, find even young kids a lot less cute compared to those who typically only see a few kids per day. When young kids congregate as they do at school, the shallow nature of cuteness is exposed; 100 nine-year-olds are not so cute, especially when they are screaming, whining, not listening and being generally uncooperative.

At the societal level, however, our view of kids, a label we typically impose on those ages 6 to 10 roughly, is still relatively positive, with cuteness outweighing the hassles associated with taking care of them, watching over them and setting them straight when they misbehave. There are some keeners even in this age group, however, who already set themselves apart definitively as not cute. These are the ones who make "trouble" that is "deeply concerning" to the adults. They tend to make a lot of trouble, care little about the consequences and thrive on negativity. From the societal point of view, we maintain some concern for these kids and we engage professional services to deal with their "deeply concerning" behaviors; deep down we hope that they can be fixed. At the institutional level, and especially in schools, these kids become subject to early prognoses: they are the future criminals, deviants, and homeless people who certainly won't finish school; they won't develop wholesome skills; and they most certainly won't be welcomed into our homes to visit our own children.

Everything changes as young people become teenagers. Teenagers are not cute; or at least they are not usually cute. Between acne and existential angst, self-esteem problems and the need to impress peers, hygiene issues, and biologically driven laziness, teenagers are arguably the least popular demographic of modern societies. Never mind that they are also the group that volunteers more than any other, that holds more progressive values than any other and that is more environmentally conscious than any other. Societal views of teenagers range from tolerable to annoying. Parental views of their teenagers differ substantially from such societal views. Parents have the luxury of having known their teenagers from birth.[2] There is a latent cuteness effect that helps parents see beyond the annoying characteristics of their teenagers;

---

[2] In blended families where new adults are introduced in parenting or quasi-parenting roles to children nearing adolescents or even to teenagers, problems between the new parent and the young person are very common and often reflect the difficulty on the part of the new parent to relate to the decidedly not cute behaviors of the young person. At the same time, the biological parent often cannot relate to the new parent's difficulties, in this respect, because that parent has access to cute memories from when the young person was a child. There is much literature about blended families; a good source in this particular context is Martin (2009), whose book details the emotional challenges for step-parents. A slightly dated, but excellent academic source, is Crosbie-Burnett & Giles-Slims (1994).

there are also circumstances where parents experience pride and joy in relation to their teenagers. Of course, the teenagers whose parents see them as their pride and joy are the ones who are compliant at home and conforming to the community. They rarely if ever cause "trouble", and when they make a mistake, it is not typically seen as "deeply concerning". These teenagers model the ideal view of citizenship; in fact, they are "better" citizens than their parents, more pure and reliably positive than their teachers, and higher performing academically and/or in sports that anyone in their extended family.

For the vast majority of teenagers, their "goodness" is largely ignored, both by society and by many of the institutions that they come into contact with. In spite of the fact that these teenagers are, for the most part, well behaved, very compliant and generally good students, and notwithstanding that most don't smoke, drink alcohol or consume drugs, they are constantly seen as bearing at least some of the responsibility for youth issues in general. "We need more youth leaders, role models, peer mentors and the like." "The reason for youth issues in our societies, communities and neighborhoods is, at least partially, that young people, or teenagers, just don't step up to the plate." "They are not taking the initiative to ensure their demographic is productive and represents good citizenship." Somehow, we manage to blame good teenagers for all sorts of issues that involve young people, and sometimes we even succeed in blaming them for issues that are fundamentally about adults (Sadeler & Gharabaghi, 2007).

Why does this happen? Because the consequence of not being cute anymore is not just an aesthetic one; as cuteness diminishes, all young people become open targets for being blamed. It is quite irrelevant whether or not this makes sense, or whether there is evidence, or even the remotest indication that young people are part of the problem. When you change from cute to not cute, you could be part of the problem, and if falsely accused, get over it. The only thing less cute than a pimple-laced, insecure, badly smelling teenager is an indignant teenager.

This, in very broad and sweeping terms, is the context in which we are going to talk about edgy youth. They are the edgy ones, among a sea of teenagers, who, at the best of times, cannot escape the adult need to lay blame, judge, label, marginalize and oppress. To be a youth is tough; to be an edgy youth ranges from extremely tough to very lonely, and from very dangerous to outright painful. Who are these edgy youth?

IN SEARCH OF THE EDGE

Our need for labels and diagnoses has led us to create categories of young people that assign health and illness, capacity and incompetence, citizenship and criminality in an attempt to differentiate the specific circumstances young people face at any given time. More importantly, it is such labels and diagnoses that have given us the foundation upon which to build a societal response to myriad issues presented by young people. Thus, we have a children's mental health system to address the needs of those young people suffering from mental health disorders such as depression, bipolar disorders or mood disorders. We have created the youth justice system, including its custodial components, to deal with young people who break the law. We have a child welfare system to ensure that young people at risk of harm are protected, and we have an education system that provides opportunities for schooling and learning to young people in all communities.

Even a cursory exploration reveals that such categorizations of young people do not reflect the reality of the everyday experiences young people have in their life space. As it turns out, young people with mental health challenges often also commit crimes, or are in need of protection, or face difficulties at school, or face all of these and many other issues for which no single institution, organization or even service sector wants to take responsibility. Indeed, there is, at all times and in every community, a group of young people who meet both the inclusion and the exclusion criteria of virtually every service sector and agency around: they have mental health issues that require the services of a children's mental health center, but they are also in need of protection, and, therefore, the children's mental health center refers them to the child welfare agency. The child welfare agency is unable to meet the mental health needs of the young person, who then acts out and, in the process, becomes aggressive toward someone, resulting in criminal charges and entry into the youth justice system. While there, the young person is excluded from mainstream schooling and attends a special school program within the custodial facility instead. Upon discharge, the young person cannot manage the social pressures of the mainstream school and gets suspended, with referrals to children's mental health, child welfare and youth justice services all going out into the hopeless abyss of "ineligibility for service".

Over time, young people pick up additional characteristics, experiences and habits that marginalize them from service systems. They might get involved with youth gangs; experiment with drugs, often leading to addictions; or sustain brain injuries resulting from fights, drug abuse, accidents, and generally unhealthy lifestyles. Sometimes, they even become parents at a very young age, creating a whole other set of issues and concerns. Many young people spend their teenage years moving from one service to another, failing at all of them, and being told that their specific circumstances just don't fit the helping systems available. Imagine the message: "You are not good enough to be helped".

In this book, I want to make the argument that there is no such thing as a young person with mental health issues, or a young person in need of protection, or one in need of educational and learning supports, and so on. All of these categorizations are little more than evidence of our collective failure to recognize, acknowledge and celebrate the humanity of a young people whose lives have unfolded outside of the norm, however defined. The young people that no service sector wants to deal with, no agency is able to contain, and no system has successfully engaged are the edgy youth this book is about. Learning how to be with these edgy youth is one of the most urgent matters in our communities and societies: our current approach of complacency toward failure and institutional irrelevance will spread from edgy youth to other groups that are easily marginalized. Our hesitation to stand on the edge is a strong indicator of the vulnerabilities of our so-called democracies.[3]

Any young person can be an edgy youth. Our first task in identifying edgy youth is to acknowledge our tendency to stereotype. Edginess is not always visible, although some young people work very hard at making it so. These are the young people whose pants are nearly around their ankles all the time, whose body piercings are in unusual places and very large, whose tattoos scream at the world. They are the young people who always seem to hang out in groups, where everyone always is smoking cigarettes, and where spitting on the ground seems as natural as taking a breath. Nonetheless, not all young people who look edgy are, in fact, edgy. Unbeknown to the passerby, many of these youth attend school during the day, come home and check in with their middle class parents and are out there with permission from their parents. They will act edgy while with their peers, trying to outdo one another, but

---

[3] A good example of how a lack of capacity to be with a particular social group can threaten the fundamental premise of democracies is the experience of indigenous peoples around the world. In my home country, Canada, for example, the colonialism was never really mitigated by the colonial populations learning how to be with the aboriginal population, and as a result, even today, we have aboriginal peoples and communities living entirely separate and profoundly marginalized lives from the dominant societies and communities. In cities and in rural areas, white people, in particular, are unable to live with the First Nations, who find themselves severely marginalized and alienated from the democratic process and political institutions. An excellent history of First Nations in Canada is Dickason, O.P. & McNab, D.T. (2002).

eventually they will go home, and do some homework and go to bed, not before kissing their moms or dads good night.

Physical appearance and outward behavior are poor indicators of edginess. I remember asking a teenager with a punk appearance about his reasons for being a punk. "I am protesting", he said, "the violence of the corporation, the abuse of children and the bullshit fed to us by the media." This particular teenager was not edgy; he was trendy, as evidenced by the Tommy Hilfiger jeans, the Nike running shoes and the ear buds that appeared to be permanently embedded in his ears. Clearly in his protest, he had not yet found the time to read Naomi Klein's *No Logo*; if anything, he was the poster boy for the very things against which he claimed to be protesting.

Another challenge to our stereotyping rests in the belief that edgy youth can be identified by their behavior. Edgy youth, in this school of thought, are essentially very poorly behaved young people. It is true, of course, that many edgy youth are indeed badly behaved. Many smoke, drink alcohol, consume drugs, have unprotected sex with multiple partners, commit at least petty crimes quite often, and even become violent, particularly in the context of intimate relationships. But this list of behaviors does not capture all the edgy youth. There are some edgy youth who are not badly behaved at all: they don't smoke or do drugs; they don't commit crimes; and they don't become violent, especially not in intimate relationships because very often, they just don't have such relationships. But they are still very different from the "average teenager"; they are "loners", "nerds", disengaged from one and all, seemingly always tense and unpredictable; to be frank, they scare the crap out of us, even though they are generally doing nothing wrong. [4]

Behavior can be misleading in another context as well. After all, many teenagers who we don't think of as edgy at all, perhaps because of their average performance in school; their abstinence from smoking, drugs and alcohol; and their lack of involvement in sexual activity, are nevertheless very badly behaved. They lie and manipulate, they are demanding and ungrateful, and generally contribute nothing to their society, community or family. Regardless, their behavior is tolerated largely because when it is ignored, no harm to anyone in particular is apparent.

There is a third stereotype of edgy youth that is worth considering. This is the well-intended, poor kid, bleeding heart stereotype that sometimes emerges from very complex articulations of social justice, social democracy, anti-

---

[4] The coverage and post-crisis event analysis of incidents such as the Columbine school shooting in the United States are often very unhelpful. See for example Cullen, D. (2009).

oppression and human rights perspectives. Edgy youth within these perspectives are defined not on the basis of their own being, but rather based on their social context and experiences of growing up. Thus, we cite poverty, abuse, neglect, marginalization, racism, victimization, and the like as the causes of edginess, and we develop social justice responses to their edginess that focus on making up for the injustice of their earlier experiences.

These perspectives, however, are just as limited in their definitions of edgy youth as all the others. In fact, many edgy youth have not had any of these difficult experiences. They hail from a middle class, dominant race, and families of positive values where there was no trace of abuse, neglect or wrong doing of any kind. Yet still, by the time they hit their teenage "not so cute anymore" phase, they stray from the middle class path toward mediocrity and become special; special in an edgy sort of way.

We can conclude, thus far, that edgy youth cannot be defined based on the obvious stereotypes; neither their physical appearance, nor their behavior, nor their social context alone provides enough information and a sufficiently reliable context in which edginess can be constructed. Edgy youth can be none or all of these things. For most of us, edgy youth are situated in relation to trouble; we can imagine edgy youth as being troubled, in trouble, troubling to others or trouble for others. For the youth being discussed here, the concept of "trouble" reflects their marginalization. For many, "trouble" is just another way of acknowledging that there is something different about them, something noteworthy, something special. Situating them in relation to trouble affords society the opportunity to ignore this specialness, this uniqueness.

I am using the term edgy youth specifically in order to avoid the various stereotypes and associations with trouble that are so often imposed on young people who are different and unique. And I am using this term, also, to be inclusive of young people whose public personas vary considerably, ranging from the violent, rough and scary character we avoid on the streets to the quiet, gentle and often scared character who works incredibly hard at being invisible. A good way of thinking about edgy youth, therefore, is to imagine a gathering of people on a plateau. There are all kinds of different people, representing different ages, different social roles, different economic contexts, different cultures and so on. At the center of the plateau we find many different kinds of buildings that house our core institutions, such as: governments, schools, jails, and sports clubs. Also toward the center we find private institutions, such as: shopping malls, grocery stores, private clubs and even private residences. People are everywhere around these buildings, walking, talking, laughing or just rushing around. As we look toward the edges of the plateau, however, we find young people just loitering, hovering near the edge; sometimes in groups and sometimes alone. They interact primarily with one another, but from time to time can't help but glance toward the center of the plateau. Perhaps they do so to keep up with what is going on there; or perhaps they do so because they dream of becoming part of that center. Most of these young people spend their time near the edge of the plateau, but at a safe enough distance to be only marginally at risk of falling over. Some of them are closer to the edge than others, and occasionally, one will indeed fall over, although it is never quite clear whether that was the intent or whether other circumstances unwittingly brought him or her closer to the edge to the point of stepping beyond it (Beautrais, 2003).

The metaphor of the plateau may give the impression that edgy youth experience a singular form of marginalization, or that they are being pushed to the periphery of the social scene in a straight forward and dichotomous manner. In fact, this is not the case. Edgy youth find themselves on the edges of many different plateaus, including the plateaus of their family, school, neighborhood, culture and identity. All of these are places within their life space; that space where their lives unfold every day. It is the accumulated effect of being pushed to the edge on all of these different plateaus that ultimately lands them on the edge of their life space plateau: the grand plateau of life with its cute, democratized fascism at the center, and its ugly, disordered anarchism around the edges. Looking back toward the center from their perspective on the edge, these youth experience envy and scorn, love and hatred, pain and pleasure. To the extent that they must, they might reach out into the center and grab what they need. But to the extent that the center reaches out to them, in the hopes of pulling them away from the edge to some undetermined place of social and personal irrelevance within the center, they respond, individually and collectively, with a determined, compelling and altogether offensive, "f@ck you".

A VIEW FROM THE EDGE

While we have spent an extraordinary amount of time "viewing" edgy youth as they live their lives on the edge, it is noteworthy that we have spent almost no time at all trying to understand how edgy youth see us from their perspective. Our own efforts to observe edgy youth in their habitat have resulted in myriad representations of life on the edge. At the level of popular culture, we might think of *Rebels Without a Cause* as a defining moment in the history of representing edgy youth. In that movie, edgy youth are represented as moody, risk-taking, irresponsible, self-conscious, irrational, emotional and yet somehow still admirable in their attempts to help one another. The movie did not sugar coat the severity of issues, and in the end, the opportunity to be admired for one of the youth required the accidental, or perhaps unnecessary death of another youth as context. Twenty years later, the movie *Grease* represented edgy youth in similar ways, except with a much more pronounced sexual component and without the seriousness and realism of *Rebels Without a Cause*. Edgy youth in that movie really were goofy youth, although some of the themes were hardly goofy, including repeated school failure, unprotected sex, and the ridiculously unflattering representation of women throughout the movie.

In literature, the classic representation of edgy youth is surely J. D. Salinger's *The Catcher in the Rye*. Holden Caulfield, the novel's protagonist, is represented not only as an edgy youth in the context of what he does, but perhaps more substantively so in the context of what he thinks. This representation of an edgy youth is arguably the most comprehensive attempt to glean a view from the edge; in fact, one might be hard pressed to find a more comprehensive and fitting attempt, even in academic literature. Holden's epic weekend described in the novel follows the metaphor of the plateau; the novel starts with Holden, literally on the edge of the year-end football game played between two private high schools. Throughout the novel, he is on the edge of his family, connecting to get what he needs but rejecting anything else that is offered. Much of his activity throughout the weekend is on the edge of the New York night scene, never really finding his place anywhere but quickly moving in and out of several places.

Still, Holden is, after all, a fictional character and, therefore, the invention of his author. As far as real edgy youth are concerned, what they see when they look at us, or from the edge toward the center, remains somewhat of a mystery. Certainly we have not spent a great deal of time asking for them to explain or articulate what they see. Instead, we have, with increasing frequency in recent years, invited edgy youth to help us develop programs and services that might be helpful to them in terms of transitioning from the edge to the center. We even have a term for this: youth engagement. Youth engagement typically entails a thinly disguised attempt to give legitimacy to adult-designed and operated initiatives by having some carefully selected young people endorse what is being offered. Funders and policymakers are then treated to a parade of young people who are said to be benefitting from the wonderful programs and services created by a particular organization or agency.

Not all youth engagement is like this. There are examples of more authentic forms of youth engagement across North America, the UK, and Europe, but many of these initiatives are seen as the exception. Indeed, the fact that it are these kinds of exceptional programs that typically win prizes and awards for their originality and commitment to youth really confirms authenticity in the context of youth engagement as the exception, rather than the norm.

We cannot learn very much about what edgy youth might see when looking toward the center from inauthentic approaches to youth engagement. Instead, we must rely on their comments and contributions on the fly, informally, and without prompting, or as part of their conversations with people who have found ways to connect with them. Based on my own connections with young people and edgy youth, in particular, I can offer my perspective on what I think edgy youth see while viewing the center. The first important observation about what they might see is that they do not reject, dismiss or ridicule everything. Quite to the contrary, most edgy youth are connected to the center, albeit often in fragile and unreliable ways. For example, youth with significant street involvement, nevertheless still have family that they continue to be in touch with. They also use street outreach services, spend time in some of the business establishments of the center, and often maintain relationships with individuals firmly embedded within the center. Many edgy youth quite like elements of the center and search for ways of accessing these without altogether coming off the edge.

A second observation about what edgy youth see when looking toward the center is a degree of disbelief about the trivialities and superficialities of the center. Edgy youth have much more experience with a critical engagement of contemporary societal structures and processes. Therefore, most also have much more nuanced and philosophically sophisticated understandings of the everyday unfolding of life at the center. Perhaps, most importantly, these young people have had to think about how they fit into myriad societal structures and processes. As a result, they have a strongly developed sense of self, at least inasmuch as they are able to provide an image of this Self to the outside world (within themselves, this sense of Self often turns out to be much more fragile that the outwardly presentation of Self).

Third, edgy youth are often generally much more optimistic than young people, and certainly more so than adults concerned about edgy youth. By optimistic, I mean specifically that edgy youth can imagine themselves defying the odds of various adversities, even when there is clear evidence of this being extremely unlikely. School failure, drug addiction and criminal records are no reason to despair; edgy youth belief that these kinds of minor hiccups can be overcome, a new life can be started and progress toward personal growth and success can be swift. Typically, these young people are bored by the negativity of the center, which tends to make a pretty big deal out of success at school, abstinence from drugs and rejection of crime.

Fourth and finally, edgy youth are very much in tune with the hypocrisy of much of what happens within the center. They can readily identify the hypocritical pronouncements of religious institutions that preach kindness but promote religious wars; they can point to the hypocrisy of environmentalism from the air conditioned front seat of a V8 SUV. They can readily see the abuse and neglect of elders in western societies, while at the same time mid-aged adults preach respect for them; they understand that values such as loyalty, commitment, caring and sharing are to be upheld only so long as there is profit associated with these. The list is endless, and edgy youth are very much focused on these kinds of issues as a way of legitimizing and rationalizing their distance from the center, and their place on the edge of emotional safety and comfort.

THE DISENGAGEMENT RESPONSE

What are young people to do when everything associated with convenience and safety seems somehow disconnected from their day-to-day experiences, but life on the edge is not particularly satisfying either? This question gets to the heart of the matter rather quickly and abruptly. Since we have already brought up the concept of hypocrisy, let us not forget the ultimate hypocrisy in the lives of edgy youth: virtually all of the dynamics in the center that are viewed as hypocritical are replicated and sometimes accentuated on the edge. Edgy youth cannot escape the reality that their edginess really does nothing to improve or modify whatever it is they are being edgy about. They, too, live their lives through the center, albeit physically they live it on the edge.

In the absence of a better way, edgy youth do what anyone does who gets annoyed but is unable to resolve their own annoyance – they disengage. Disengagement is a strategic response in times of uncertainty. It serves the purpose of rendering any meaningful response to a situation unnecessary, and instead moves along with a declaratory commitment to avoidance and not caring. Edgy youth are masters at the disengagement response, and are able to not only disengage in real time and space, but also to re-imagine themselves engaging in a new social context, often one that is constituted through virtual technologies.[5]

Disengagement strategies are really a hopeless attempt to either overplay one's distaste for the center, or to pretend one is barely aware of its existence. We tend to be particularly aware of those edgy youth who choose the first option, and who we see parading around in unique clothes: they are the smokers, drinkers, druggies, obnoxiously vulgar youth that are commonly seen in the downtown cores of larger cities, but increasingly also in the coffee shops of smaller towns. As we discussed earlier, these are the youth we like to label based on their appearance, their behavior and perhaps also the simple fact that we see them loitering in town when they really ought to be at school. Unwittingly, as long as we maintain our safe distance and our desperate efforts to walk around them, to ignore their behavior, to pretend we are not bothered, the more we reinforce their disengagement. Their efforts to be "other", to be misfits, are rewarded with our efforts to avoid them.

There are also edgy youth who take a less visible approach to life on the edge. Their disengagement with the center is much more literal. They try to blend in so as to maintain their invisibility. They are quiet, removed, and almost shy in social contexts and in public spaces. We barely notice these youth, even though they are almost always present in the malls we frequent, at school, in community centers and throughout the downtown core.

Perhaps, it is not obvious why edgy youth work so hard to disengage from the center. There are, after all, other options, including rebelling against the center, advocating on their own behalf, or turning to crime and violence to ensure their own economic survival (some do, but most don't). One reason why edgy youth prefer disengagement over some of these alternatives is that in the process of recognizing their own edginess and moving their lives toward the edge, it becomes increasingly difficult for them to see any relevance in engaging the center; their way of being, as far as a they can tell, is simply not reflected anywhere in the center, whereas it is easily reflected and non-judgmentally accepted on the edge. Working toward change within the center, on the other hand, threatens this escape route. If the center really did open doors for edgy youth to enter and re-integrate, where would they go if they needed to leave again? A center that expands to include its edges is malignant;

---

[5] This is evident in the ever-evolving complexity of character development in gaming and identity formation in social networking.

like suburbs, such a center swallows difference and uniqueness and replaces it with a near-totalitarian approach to sameness and cultural hegemony.[6]

THE BROTHERHOOD AND SISTERHOOD OF EDGY YOUTH

One of the more peculiar aspects of edgy youth is their ability to find one another; where we encounter one edgy youth, we typically don't have to look too hard or wait too long to find another. This is perhaps not surprising when we think of edgy youth who work hard to be visible. These youth are often excluded from the center's institutions; dismissed from social gatherings; and expelled, even from universal services such as education and health care. These youth often find each other at the court house, the police station or in alternative residential settings, such as: group homes, youth shelters, treatment centers or custody facilities. Since most of these kinds of settings typically don't allow access to non-edgy youth, or youth who are found ineligible for entry or admission on the grounds of being "too good", edgy youth who find themselves frequenting or living in such places really have access only to youth who, like them, are also edgy. The common experience of being excluded; of being given subtle and sometimes very overt messages of rejection; and of being labeled "disordered", "criminal", "deviant" or "disturbed" certainly helps to create a sense of brotherhood or sisterhood. Disengagement from the center is a lot more fun in peer groups than when one has to maintain such isolation alone.

Perhaps, more difficult to understand is the coming together of edgy youth who work hard to be invisible. Many of these youth are not frequent visitors at the court house or in institutional residential settings, and they somehow still manage to limit their social relations to youth who, like them, are edgy in a quiet, removed sort of way. What this means is that edgy youth have the capacity to *recognize* one another, often well before anyone else is able to identify them as edgy. As it turns out, most settings where youth gather have a good representation of edgy youth. Nowhere is this more the case than in schools, where we are only starting to acknowledge the scale of edginess. While our initial reactions to incidents, such as the Columbine school shootings, were limited to identifying reasons for the exceptionality of the youth responsible, we now know that these were not really as exceptional as

---

[6] In the context of suburbanization, this process is brilliantly laid out by James Kunzler (1993) in his *Geography of Nowhere.*

one might have thought. Current estimates of mental health concerns, addictions, and other exceptionalities range from 25% to 50% of the student population in schools across North America, not including learning disabilities and undiagnosed developmental issues (Kutash, Duchnowski & Lynn, 2006).

As it turns out, group dynamics among youth are such that the characteristics of edginess are easily identified by those who know them all too well: the actual edgy youth. The nuances of exclusion, victimization at the hand of bullies, anxiety barely contained, and of that indeterminate sinking feeling that all is not well are difficult to make out for those merely trained in their identification and assessment; these nuances are glaring and quite obvious to make out for those who actually carry their burden every day.

There is safety and comfort in finding one another on the edge. It is a lonely place, after all, and not nearly as hustling and bustling as the center. Stepping off the everyday activity of the center can be overwhelming, and the deafening silence of the edge can be scary. The stress of second guessing whether the right moves have been made, whether the future is promising, whether there is any point in going on is much more bearable when shared with others in similar predicaments. The brotherhoods and sisterhoods of edgy youth are about reassurance, confirmation and rationalization. They reassure each brother or sister that they are not alone and that their path to the edge is a path well traveled; in other words, they are not weird. Confirmation is granted to those who question their decisions and their current state of isolation from the center. The decisions were good decisions, because suggesting that they were bad decisions would implicate all the brothers and sisters as poor decision-makers. Finally, rationalizing the struggles associated with the edge is an on-going project, since the evidence of benefits is usually pretty thin. Nevertheless, there is no shortage of rationalizations for why being an edgy youth is necessary. Critiques of the center, and the rejection imposed on these youth by the center, are relatively easy to articulate. In fact, these critiques are usually accurate. The one thing, perhaps, that is not entirely accurate or true is that rejection must be greeted with disengagement. The brotherhood and sisterhood of edgy youth might be just slightly guilty of overly simplistic generalizations, hiding other options associated with dealing with the rejection from the center. For the time being, however, hanging on to the edge is better than losing it.

EDGY YOUTH WHO LOSE THEIR EDGE

Most edgy youth experience some very interesting things during their teenage years, but begin to gradually reacquaint themselves with the center as they enter adulthood. Some of the edgiest youth around make the transition to citizen and responsible adult in their young adulthood and end up becoming leaders in the center for years to come. Most edgy youth simply fade into "normalcy" and a lack of exceptionality; by the time they reach mid-adulthood, one can no longer distinguish them from anyone else. Some of these individuals cannot maintain their own history of edginess even as a memory; they erase their edginess (sometimes we mistakenly think of this as resilience).

Some edgy youth, on the other hand, lose their edge altogether and these are the ones to whom we really must pay careful attention. Some edgy youth die on the edge, often at their own hands, and sometimes as victims of situations or circumstances that have spun out of control. Others may physically survive their edgy teenage years but never recover from the trauma or adversity faced during those years. These individuals become very ill and incapacitated as they enter adulthood and their path through life is characterized not by the pride and freedom associated with getting there on their own, but by the pain and suffering associated with becoming a chronic invalid (taken literally, a person who is not valid in the spectrum of humanity). Again others, unfortunately quite a number of others, enter adulthood with severe restrictions on their edginess; they end up in jail for many, many years for crimes that exceeded society's tolerance for edginess.

There are many different reasons why edgy youth might lose their edge; for every young person there is a different story. We can, however, make some general observations about what might have happened to those who really lost their edge. First, it is very likely that just like these edgy youth disengaged from the center in order to find their place on the edge, they also disengaged from the edge, but this time with nowhere else left to find a place except beyond the edge where there is only nothingness. Second, it is very likely that these youth were disappointed by life on the edge; whatever it is they expected to find they were unable to find and they lost hope that they would ever find it. Third, these youth were not challenged in a meaningful and substantive manner about their place on the edge and their relationship with the center. Their connections with elements of the center were simply insufficient right from the start. Finally, these youth were rejected by the brotherhood or sisterhood of the edge, because these brotherhoods and sisterhoods, although very important and helpful in some respects, can also be cruel and violent in other respects.

LIFE ON THE EDGE

Before we go too far in describing life on the edge, it is important to make a nuanced distinction between living on the edge and being an edgy youth. These two concepts are not the inevitable products of one another. It is entirely possible to spend much time on the edge without actually being edgy, and it is also possible to fake one's presence in the center, while really being quite edgy. Yet, the distinction between life on the edge and being edgy is indeed nuanced: when we remember that we are using the spatial concepts of edge and center metaphorically, we can acknowledge that young people who perceive their lives to be unfolding on the edge are indeed edgy, and conversely, young people who fake their life in the center are simply constructing a differently located edge within other people's idea of the center.

What we really want to ensure is that we don't confuse edgy behavior with being edgy. There are many young people who do things that they shouldn't, or things that might, by parental standards, be considered edgy. This might include: smoking, drug and alcohol use, sexual activity, and even petty crimes. These things, however, are not by themselves symptomatic of being an edgy youth; these are simply behaviors that might be exploratory, the result of boredom, the succumbing to peer pressure under particular circumstances, or reflective of impulsive decision-making without really considering the consequences.

Life on the edge is not about the occasional behavioral or situational activities of young people. Instead, it is about the everyday activities of those young people we can reasonably consider to be edgy youth. Their everyday activities are not exclusive to poor behavior, but also include very positive behaviors; the negotiation of relatively complex value systems; and a rich but often very complicated internal life of the mind, the imagination and the soul. While every edgy young person lives life in his or her very own unique and special way, there are several characteristics of life on the edge that we can identify, likely having a place in every, or at least most, edgy youth's lives. First, among these characteristics, is the lack of externally imposed structure. This is a very challenging dilemma for edgy youth: part of being edgy is to resist imposed structures. Resistance is a context of forming an identity and purpose, and most edgy youth spend considerable time and effort strengthening their resistance to all things imposed. This is not necessarily a bad thing; many of the things they resist they do so with clarity of mind, excellent judgment and social justice on their side. The challenge is that when resisting externally imposed structure, they also give up some very useful tools for organizing their life. Where many young people really can move through much of their day almost robotically, with few major decision-making requirements and with most basic needs supplied as they go, edgy youth forgo this luxury and have to work to re-create each day as it comes their way. It is never obvious that they need to get out of bed in the morning, then have breakfast, get ready for school and actually go to school. Even if they physically attend at school, it is not obvious that they will attend classes, focus on what is being taught, interact with teachers, and eventually go home. Their afternoons are often completely unplanned and are structured only in real time, as opportunities for things come up and peers make contact. Who knows when it will be time for bed? A good night's sleep to get ready for the next day is never guaranteed either.

While it is common and perhaps intuitively meaningful for adults and good citizens to complain about the "laziness" of edgy youth, nothing could be further from the truth. Edgy youth work extremely hard every day to invent the program for that day, often with no resources and a great deal of unpredictability and uncertainties. A lack of structure is hard work, which is why most of us make sure that we have externally imposed structures in our lives, be that through school, jobs, recreational routines, or what-have-you.

Related to the lack of structure, edgy youth experience another dynamic in their lives that distinguishes life on the edge from life in the center. Youth who are firmly entrenched in the center believe themselves to be where they ought to be; edgy youth on the other hand, are chronically searching for something, yet it is not always clear (even to them) for what. This is one of the great ironies of being an edgy youth; young people become edgy because of their disengagement from the center as a way of abandoning their discomfort and sometimes traumatic experiences there. As soon as they set foot on the edge, however, they encounter an entirely new anxiety and discomfort that keeps them searching for something else. Edgy youth may appear exuberant, confident and happy; in fact, edgy youth are always uncomfortable and insecure. While they have worked hard through their brotherhoods and sisterhoods of edgy youth to find a place of belonging, deep down they know that they have not yet found it and that they must, for some time to come, keep searching.

Life on the edge is much more relational than life in the center. Relational, in this context, means that those living on the edge are paying attention to their relationships; they value these relationships and they are focused on the nuances of interaction, interdependence and collaboration. Edgy youth typically take nothing for granted in the context of their relationships. They are very critical, often hyper-vigilant about issues of trustworthiness, loyalty and commitment. Perhaps as a result of previous disappointments, edgy youth have low expectations of others in the context of relationships, but they have high hopes that others will prove them wrong. In other words, edgy youth crave relationships that make them feel good, strong and happy; however, each young person might define these things differently.[7] Along with relationships, edgy youth also have an exaggerated approach to boundaries, either by maintaining very strict barriers so as to avoid disappointment or alternatively, by becoming accessible to others without any discernible limits or conditions. Edgy youth often lack experience in the creation of boundaries and they have rarely been invited to co-create their boundaries with others (adults or persons of authority) (Stuart, 2008).

Edgy youth are often wise beyond their age. This is both their greatest asset as well as somewhat of a liability. Their wisdom provides much ammunition for their rejection of and disengagement from the center. Much of what edgy youth wish to protest, in fact, deserves protesting. Much of what they perceive as unjust is indeed unjust. Most edgy youth are able to recognize the shallow and superficial nature of adult interventions and attempts to recruit them back to the center. Indeed, edgy youth are very, very good at assessing the competence of those seeking to connect with them, change them, cure them, discipline them or bring them "home". They are quite right in concluding that most systems, institutions, professionals and concerned adults are not really very competent in their specific context. Almost everything these "helpers" or "interveners" do is really just made up stuff of little relevance to the everyday life of edgy youth.

This kind of wisdom is useful in many situations, and edgy youth can take pride in having figured out the futility and trivialities of modern life. The disadvantage, however, is that edgy youth become stuck in a place where

---

[7] The centrality of relationship in the lives of young people is not only a social phenomenon but finds confirmation in what has been termed "relationship science". Much effort to incorporate brain sciences into our understanding of being with edgy youth is yielding interesting results. While more research is needed, there is clarity and near-consensus among researchers that building a relationship foundation when engaging young people is absolutely necessary. See for example Berscheid (1999).

moving forward or exploring alternatives requires them to be at least somewhat responsive to those systems, institutions or professionals that they have already deemed incompetent. Some edgy youth are able to do this; many are not.

A TIME AND PLACE FOR EDGY YOUTH

It is important to get passed the momentary image of edginess presented by youth hanging out, looking rough and talking tough. In fact, edgy youth have a complicated relationship with time and place. They bring together in the here and now a past, a present and a future that seem oddly incompatible and sometimes quite depressing. Many edgy youth can tell difficult stories about bad things that have happened to them in the past; such things might include abuse, neglect or abandonment, and sometimes it includes all three of these. Even young people who did not necessarily have these experiences within their families or immediate social communities can nevertheless often cite these kinds of things in their more recent past, with abuse and neglect usually occurring at the hands of peers rather than caregivers. At the very least, edgy youth can tell the story of a past in which they felt out of place, either because others in their social context told them so with little nuance ("get out of my house you f@cking bastard") or because they discovered that some of their identity was too different from their social context to have any chance of finding acceptance (often in the context of sexual identity, but also developmental identity – some youth are too smart for their social context).

Such stories from the past are never fully resolved. No amount of therapy, treatment or professional intervention can recreate the past to render these experiences absent. At best, the impact of such experiences can be mitigated, the capacity on the part of young people to function well in society in spite of these experiences can be increased or reinforced, and the social context of young people can be motivated to become more inviting and open to the uniqueness of young people that might previously have simply been rejected. Nonetheless, the past is still there; these experiences are forever carried forward by edgy youth, each managing this past in their own unique (and almost never consistently forward-looking) manner.

The past is not, however, the only time or even the dominant time for edgy youth. Whatever the status of past experiences, there is the present to contend with and new experiences are being added onto the past that require focus and attention of the young people right now. Edgy youth accumulate major experiences very rapidly. Such experiences include sexual encounters that move far more quickly than they should from interest to implementation; for girls especially, such encounters often expose girls not only to sexual possibilities, but also to new ways of being oppressed, violated and dismissed. Relationships, in general, are being experienced as critical elements of life on the edge, and identities are evolving in tandem with such relationship experiences. Decisions about drugs, alcohol and participation in criminal activity all need to be made quickly and repeatedly, in many cases daily.

Some experiences and decisions in the present are congruent with those from the past; in other words, we can easily see the continuity from past to present. Edgy youth are not quite this predictable all the time, however, and often we find that what is happening in the present really is not at all congruent with the past, and there is little continuity between past and present. The intuitive conclusion that difficulties or challenges in the present are inherently and always connected to issues of abuse, victimization or other sorts of challenges in the past is, at the very least, speculative. More likely, such a conclusion is simply wrong, at least some of the time. Edgy youth have faced challenges in the past and are facing challenges in the present, and while past and present are connected, the specific challenges they face may or may not be.

Once we move beyond the past and present and focus on the future, the situation of edgy youth becomes further complicated. Their future is largely undetermined and any prognosis based on past or current troubles tends to be weak and often entirely wrong. Certainly, the future as edgy youth imagine it looks quite bright. Most of these young people maintain a very optimistic view of what might be possible as time passes, and they believe themselves to be capable of getting away from the less attractive features of life on the edge. Indeed, many edgy youth are successful in doing just that. As it turns out, many of our most successful and upstanding citizens in Canada and the US turn out to have very edgy histories, including stints in detention and foster care as well as heavy street-involvement, drug use, violence and the like.[8]

When edgy youth manage to shape a future that is fundamentally distinct from their edgy past we often associate their movement with the presence of resilience. There is value to this approach, especially as we more closely examine some of the common factors that young people moving out from the

---

[8] Some notable famous people with edgy youth status at some stage in their lives include Angelina Jolie (self harming, gothic lifestyle, drug and alcohol abuse), Marilyn Monroe (moved around between foster homes, drug use) and Mike Tyson (traumatized by bullying at school, depression and self-esteem problems as well as major violence and physical assaults).

edge might have experienced. In the resilience literature we find references to community and family support, strong value systems, multiple peer groups, high self-esteem and many more that apparently contribute to the resilience of young people and render their future success as citizens more likely (Liebenberg & Ungar, 2008; Ungar, 2005). It is not my aim to criticize or dismiss resilience theory, but it does reflect a way of thinking about young people and their futures that very much reinforces the social status quo. Resilience theory is fundamentally about the reproduction of adult ways of being; thinking and doing; and, not surprisingly, edgy youth who abandon their edginess and begin to conform to adult expectations and norms will do relatively well in the evaluation schematic of those adults (Gharabaghi, 2009).

The question really is whether this transformation from edgy youth to responsible and conforming adult is the only, or even the best, way to form futures for edgy youth. The core argument of this book is that there are alternative ways of being with edgy youth that do not aim to simply reproduce existing values and conform to the social status quo. In this book, I really want to challenge the reader to imagine a much greater future for edgy youth than what resilience theory has provided: I want to forward the idea that the edginess of edgy youth is the very foundation of their success, not the barrier to their integration (or subjugation) into the center. Being with edgy youth creates possibilities for elevating resistance, rebellion, defiance and opposition as the core ingredients of leadership and social change.

A NEW APPROACH TO BEING WITH EDGY YOUTH

Stated succinctly, I want to develop an approach of being with edgy youth that is informed by a strong commitment to anti-authoritarian values, multiple identities, and active and on-going support for reflective non-compliance on their part. Such an approach calls for much greater and much more honest perspectives of the Self, on the part of professional helpers; on relationships; on conflict resolution; and on issues of trust, loyalty and representation. Perhaps most importantly, such an approach requires that the idea of being with edgy youth is firmly placed at the center of any intervention in the lives of these young people. Being with *is the intervention*, while treatment, pharmacological experimentation, pseudo-counseling, behavioral manipulations, or value-laden teachings and impositions of conformity and compliance are mere side effects of societal needs for control and order.

What I am suggesting is not simply a matter of endorsing the dysfunction, deviance and anti-social behaviors of edgy youth. Indeed, I believe that we have set expectations for these young people that have unfairly asked too little of them. Instead of expecting them to lead the world into better times, to be at the forefront of undoing the damage we ourselves and previous generations have done to the planet, to resolve the human need for war and violence, to find meaningful alternatives to unfettered capitalism and to restore integrity into our systems of democratic governance, we expect them to simply stop being so damn visible. We have done nothing at all to *be with edgy youth*; we have instead worked hard to force these young people to surrender their edge, to become like us, to disappear in the sea of "normalcy" and a singular identity from which we take such comfort and security.

I propose that we stop seeking the easy way, the unexceptional way, the self-affirming way. We must learn to really be with edgy youth; to challenge their use of their own exceptionalities, their uniqueness and their specialness; and to remove ourselves as Gods in their lives. We are not looking for edgy youth to become us; instead, we are looking for edgy youth to re-engage the center by changing its ways for the better.

Chapter 2

GET OVER IT!

In this chapter, I am going to shift my attention away from the edgy youth and focus instead on those who make their living by working with edgy youth. I refer to this group of people as professional helpers recognizing that what they do every day is in fact a professional endeavor, rather than charity work or a volunteer activity and also recognizing their desire to be helpful to young people. In fact, most professional helping disciplines are designed to further the process of helping others get by, improve their lives, or recover from whatever trauma or injury they may have suffered. I also like the term professional helper because it does not limit us to any particular professional or academic discipline. In reality, professional helpers represent many different disciplines that include: child and youth care practice; social work; counseling; and possibly even nursing, early childhood education and professionals with many different job designations in the education, justice, health care and social welfare sectors. Although I provide a very critical overview of the helping professions and even of professional helpers, I want to emphasize that I have been a professional helper for well over two decades and that I maintain the highest respect for many of the individuals involved in the social and health service fields. I do, however, believe very strongly that like in any other field, there are those who do exceptionally well and then there are those who ought to try a different field in order to avoid any further damage to others. Being with edgy youth, as we will see throughout this book, is no easy task, and I think that it is important to be straight about what should be required of professional helpers to effectively do their work.

Professionals assigned to work with edgy youth can get quite upset when someone questions their commitment to the youth or the validity of their approaches to working with them. It is as if the fact that they have accepted employment in the youth-serving fields stands as evidence, maybe even proof, that they are indeed committed and competent to work with these young people. It is not just a matter of their skills and qualifications; they believe with conviction that their values are also the right ones for the job, and that the very fact of their employment in these service fields somehow makes them different from the general population.

One might think that such beliefs are just silliness, or perhaps symptoms of professional arrogance. But this is not the case at all. These beliefs are very real and often reinforced by administrators in the field, by literature (not necessarily research-based literature), by professional associations and unions, and even by the general public on those occasions when we celebrate the fact that some people choose to do jobs we would not want to do under any circumstances. Comments such as, "It takes a special person to work with these youth." are not uncommon (Anglin, 2002; Krueger, 2004; Nightingale, 2000, Stuart, 2007). Social workers, child and youth care practitioners, mental health counselors and many other kinds of professionals who work with edgy youth receive accolades for their courage, their sense of social justice and their preparedness to expose themselves to the potential safety hazards and the deep disturbances presented by these young people. There is something honorable about putting oneself in a position to be exposed to the edges of society. Of course, in spite of the honor and the accolades, most of these professional roles are under-paid and under-valued on a day to day basis, and the more directly engaged with youth, the less material valuing of the honor and accolades is associated with the work. For example, social workers in child protection agencies, who typically see youth for five to ten hours per week and spend the rest of their time doing paper work, in meetings with adults or preparing for court, get paid reasonably well. Child and youth care practitioners in residential group programs, who typically spend most of their 40-hour work week directly dealing with youth, get paid less. Foster parents, who live with youth 24/7, barely get paid at all, and typically have to use whatever pay they do receive to finance the material needs of the youth.

The material challenges associated with the youth-serving professions, while scandalous on many levels, actually serve to perpetuate the myth of "specialness" that is often associated with professionals in the youth-serving fields. Clearly they cannot be in it for the money, or else they would never have agreed to do this work in the first place. The superficial people, those who don't understand these edgy youth and those who would rather lust for the almighty dollar, are to be found in the general population, not among the professionals from the youth-serving fields. The myth of the honor of social workers, child and youth care practitioners, counselors and many others has been embedded in the communal psyche. As a way of re-casting this myth from a different perspective, perhaps a good place to start is by asking, "Who are these people working with edgy youth?"

THE BANALITY OF GREATNESS

I want to start by emphasizing that many of the people I have encountered throughout the 22 years of my direct service career with edgy youth are wonderful people. These people have included myriad professional labels, including: social workers, child and youth care practitioners, psychologists, special education teachers, mental health counselors, behavioral intervention specialists and child life specialists. They have also included volunteers doing a range of things, including foster parents who are, arguably, the most deserving of the honorable status that we often bestow on human service professionals.

Being good at what one does, however, is not a sign of greatness. Just because a worker seems effective in connecting with an edgy youth, or takes an initiative to advocate for something on behalf of edgy youth, does not mean that these are extraordinary people with some prior characteristics that set them apart from the general population. For the most part, it means that they are good at their job, and perhaps even simply, that they are able to do what their job requires them to do. Very few professionals within the youth-serving fields came into the profession to live according to some honorable or amazing ideals related to social justice or equity (some did, but not many). Many of these professionals entered the social service fields because they thought they would not have to do any math on the job. Others entered because their friends suggested it. Yet others showed up at college or university having no idea what program they actually signed up for. These people are stunned when they find out that they are training to become involved with youth living on the edge (and many leave). Increasingly in recent years, young people enter training programs for youth-serving professions as preparation for teachers' college, and become youth-serving professionals because they were unsuccessful in their application to teachers' college. Indeed, the paths into the youth-serving professions are many and varied, and only a very few individuals embark on this journey, driven strictly by superior humanitarian values.

It is also notable that there is absolutely no evidence that youth-serving professionals hold any more progressive social or political values than the general population. Many of these professionals are concerned about high taxes, lax punishment for criminals and the aesthetic burden that homeless people place on the community's downtown. Some are right wing extremist who entered the field to force edgy youth into a version of citizenship that corresponds with the extreme right. Furthermore, there is today, as there has always been, a very strong faith-driven community of youth-serving professionals who are indeed driven to "save these youth from their self-destructive actions and values".

The point of this discussion about the professionals who work with edgy youth is not to discredit their work or their intentions. Instead, it is to ensure that we take into account the humanity that governs the process of being with edgy youth, including those aspects of our humanity that reflect the challenges, the tensions and the gross violations of core human principles we sometimes take for granted. Without acknowledging that these play a significant part in how we are and can be with edgy youth, we cannot construct a way of being with edgy youth that might move us forward as communities and societies that are inclusive, peaceful, growth-oriented and interesting for all of its members.

In response to the question, "Who are these professionals working with edgy youth?", I propose we answer with the most critical and perhaps outright negative response available, just to insure that we cover all the bases: they are individuals subject to the same racism, the same sexism, the same identity-dismissing, oppressive, inequitable and philosophically superficial value systems and mindsets we find in the general population. Far from being "special", or "great", professionals working with edgy youth are challenged every day not only by the circumstances of the youth, but also by their own biases and conflicting values. Managing these challenges remains, as it always has, the foundation of being with edgy youth in a way that is different from the powerful dichotomous representation of some humans as being good and others bad, some as healthy and others as sick, some as free and others as in need of containment.

There are some other myths about professionals working with edgy youth. It is commonly said, for example, that these professionals are predominantly young people who perhaps still need to find a path toward their own future. Within this myth, working with edgy youth is usually constructed as an "entry-level position", to be abandoned when the worker has accumulated some experience and is able to move into better, or real, positions within the helping professions. As it turns out, professionals in the youth-serving fields are not at all "young people". They vary considerably in age, although we do find that the average age of workers is low in those services that are ill designed and offer not only poor service, but also poor employment conditions. Other services that are well designed and offer reasonable compensation as well as everyday employment supports, including supervision and training, tend to have work forces that are within the norm of most employment sectors, in terms of age. In other words, there are many residential group programs for edgy youth, for example, where just about everyone on the full-time team is 40+ years old and has been working there for at least 10 years. However, it is true that very few people retire as youth workers when they are directly engaged with edgy youth, be that in residential or community settings. It would appear that there is an age, perhaps somewhere between 45 and 55, when most of these workers choose change and new challenges as a way of completing their careers. I have not, for example, come across a residential group program anywhere where the full team consisted of men and women in their 50s or 60s.

Another myth about youth-serving professionals is that they are predominantly female. Here again, we find that the proportion of female workers is strongly related to the type of service, and even to service philosophy. In very control-oriented settings, one finds at least as many men as women working with the youth, and in some extreme cases, such as the corrections sector, men are the majority. The more progressive and thoughtful settings and services tend to have more female employees. The formal training programs for youth workers in colleges and universities attract predominantly female students, often with a 9:1 female to male ratio. The obvious question about why this gender gap is not reflected to this extreme in the field is associated with the on-going insistence of the field to hire men, for their perceived authority (ie: their size and muscles), very often at the expense of any sort of real qualifications.

Given these rather archaic dynamics and issues in the make-up of the youth-serving professions, it is not surprising that the often proclaimed greatness of youth workers or youth-serving professionals does not quite materialize. It also explains why much of the very sophisticated literature related to the ethics and values of working with edgy youth is entirely ignored by those actually doing that work.

THE EXPERTISE TRAP

In the previous section, I worked hard to dismiss any notion that professionals in the youth-serving fields are somehow special in terms of their values or their commitments to young people. In this section, I will take this critical perspective one step further and argue that it is not only who these professionals are that is not quite as impressive as one might think, but even what they know, or the expertise they bring to the table, is rather more limited than what some would like us to think.

It may be shocking for readers to learn that much of what happens in the youth-serving fields is not based on any evidence or particularly compelling rationale. In fact, most initiatives that happen in these fields are based on intuition, some version of common sense, or simply on whatever came before. To make matters a little worse, it is likely that very few of those professionals who actually work with edgy youth face-to-face could even cite a single study that speaks to whatever it is they are doing with them. In some settings, the professionals providing the most direct services to edgy youth may or may not have any pre-service education or training in the field, and almost never do they have an on-going connection to the research field or even those publications that disseminate research results.

It is often the case, however, that the leadership of particular agencies or services makes claims about the evidence-based nature of their services. They cite research findings and are fluently able to speak the language of evidence-based practices. They are the ones who cement the "expertise" of the professionals in changing the lives of edgy youth. They are the ones who pave the path and allow us to walk on it. Furthermore, they are also the ones who have no business claiming any sort of expertise in this context, since most of them virtually have never interacted with edgy youth and, therefore, have not the slightest clue about what actually happens moment-to-moment when one tries to be with edgy youth.

The role of expertise while being with edgy youth is surprisingly difficult to nail down. It seems that neither those who offer evidence on how to change edgy youth nor those who work every day to force edgy youth into conformity and compliance really have any expertise in being with edgy youth. In fact, their expertise would seem to cover just about everything *except* being with edgy youth. They can speak with authority about behavior, addictions, mental health concerns, program interventions, containment, compliance, conformity, performance and a host of other "outputs" on the part of youth, but they cannot say anything at all about being with edgy youth. Sometimes we do get some lame suggestions that being with edgy youth requires a relationship, so that we can then use that relationship to break down the resistance of the youth, plow through any barriers and begin the process of imposing our values and expectations on the young person. This use of relationship confirms what expertise the professionals really do bring to the table: this is the expertise required to consolidate oppression and forced compliance.

The critique of expertise in the youth-serving professions may give the impression that there is no meaningful research unfolding at all; nothing could be further from the truth. In fact, in recent years there has been a major acceleration of research efforts related to the challenges faced by youth-serving professionals and the agencies they work for. We now have excellent research findings about all kinds of different things that relate to helping young people struggling with myriad issues in their lives. We know more about effective practices in children's mental health, child welfare, youth justice and the homeless sector than ever before. Methodologically, most of this research is very sound, conforming to standard research practices in the social sciences.[1] Indeed, except for altogether outright dismissals of positivist research approaches, most observers agree that this research has resulted in great value being added to the youth-serving professions and fields more generally.

The difficulty with research is that it can only ever answer the questions which we choose to ask; even then, it can only provide answers that will prove to be inherently wrong for some. It is important to reflect on this a little bit in order to understand why we must do better than rely on research pursuant to specific intervention approaches when it comes to edgy youth. The first issue, as mentioned, is that research is a response to specific questions. We might ask, for example, what sort of intervention might work to ensure that youth living in foster homes perform well in schools, given that currently most do not perform well in schools and many do not graduate from high school when they age-out of the care system. Researchers love these kinds of questions and are very good at seeking meaningful answers. They will conduct random experimental trials and offer particular interventions to some youth, other interventions to other youth, and no intervention at all to yet another group of youth. They will measure the academic performance of all of these young

---

[1] Several academic journals have made significant efforts in recent years to provide bridges between theory and practice, research and application. Good examples include *Relational Child and Youth Care Practice*, an independent journal out of Vancouver Island University in Canada as well as *Child & Youth Services*, a journal I co-edit and that is owned by Taylor & Francis.

people before and after the intervention, and based on who experiences the greatest positive change, they will be able to answer the question. In no time at all, we can then find out that one effective intervention for these young people is to provide them with tutoring in the foster home, ideally by the foster parents (Flynn, Marquis, Paquet & Peeke, 2011). So far, so good, but this brings us to the second issue: these results will benefit, on average, about three quarters of the young people who receive the tutoring, and there is really no way of knowing which three quarters will benefit and which quarter will not. Moreover, the intervention requires that the young person is actually present regularly enough in the foster home in order to receive it, and for long enough in order to get the full benefit over time. Edgy youth, unfortunately, rarely meet those requirements. If they did, we would no longer think of them as edgy, given that they clearly would have found their place in the center (in this case, in a licensed and regulated substitute family in the center).

I want to be clear that I support research in the youth-serving professions and fields. Furthermore, I believe that many young people and their families have benefitted immeasurably from programs and services that have been informed by research findings. The problem with virtually all research, however, is its exclusion of the everyday realities of edgy youth. Most research designs require the human subject participants to conform to at least some very basic expectations. These might relate to being present in a particular program, or it might be about their preparedness to provide feedback when prompted. Regardless of what is required, edgy youth almost never meet such requirements. This is why they are edgy. We can say whatever we want about research, but fundamentally, most research is firmly rooted in the center of society. Especially positivist research designs that operate on center assumptions and value systems are mostly administered by center-based academic institutions and are funded by center-based government agencies or private foundations. Most research is expected to yield findings that can be applied to practice in such a way that the outcomes for young people change for the better, based on the values and expectations of the center. We are not typically able to request research funding to address this kind of question: "Please tell us how to be with edgy youth."

So, what does all of this mean, in relation to the expertise we bring to the table when working with young people? It means that we have considerable expertise in shaping the growth, learning and maturing of young people who won't resist our approaches, values and expectations too much or too violently. However, we have no expertise at all about what to do with those young people who do resist, who push us to a place where we no longer feel safe and where we feel embarrassed about having our incompetence exposed. This is why edgy youth are usually left to their own devices, unless they cause problems for the center, in which case they are forcibly contained for a period of time. This is also why North Americans tend to jail edgy youth at rates that are double, and sometimes triple, those in Europe and even parts of South America and Africa.

THE NEED FOR COMPLIANCE

If only edgy youth did what we wanted them to do, so much progress could be made so much more quickly. In fact, if everyone just did what they were asked to do, we could very quickly eliminate all kinds of annoying problems in everyday life. Employees would no longer need unions or rights since they would just do what the employer asked them to do. Citizens really would not need constitutions or human rights since they would just do whatever the rules demanded. In the youth-serving professions, we have developed some really fantastically democratic language, including references to youth engagement, youth empowerment, children's rights, and principles of personalized services that include such things as voice and choice for youth and families when receiving services (Stuart & Gharabaghi, 2010). This language does represent many good ideas, and I don't want to suggest that it is entirely empty rhetoric. I do, however, want to suggest that these "service ideals" compete with a much more deeply embedded concept that almost always takes precedent over these democratic ideals. This is the concept of compliance.

Compliance simply means that those with less power listen to and act upon the wishes of those with more power. Not all compliance has to lead to profound injustice, but almost all profound injustices have required a degree of compliance (usually under the threat of force and violence) on the part of those who were made to comply. Indeed, it has been a refusal to comply, or non-compliance, that has, in many cases, put an end to injustice. The civil rights movement in the United States is one good example of this; as is the resistance to the Apartheid regime of South Africa; the collapse of the Communist Party in the Soviet Union; and as I write this, the many fights for regime change in Libya, Egypt, Yemen, Syria, Tunisia and Bahrain.

Aside from the arena of world politics, the focus on compliance has found a steady place in the intervention literature pursuant to young people facing many challenges. Residential care systems in the United States and Canada have many historical examples of the worst kind of compliance situations. In the US, a number of boarding schools for "deviant youth" turned out to be violent and fascist places of horror (Szalavitz, 2006), and in Canada, over a century of residential schools for aboriginal peoples has left a legacy of shame and broken lives that had moved across generations (Bays, 2009). Both of these examples reflect publically endorsed examples of compliance-based approaches to change people: deviant youth in the US, and barbaric Indians in Canada. In both cases, it turned out that it was the service providers and/or the state that needed intervention for their deviant and barbaric approaches associated with treating other humans.

It is always easy to discuss compliance when only in the context of social experiments, now recognized as wrong and for which apologies have been issued. Doing so would mask the reality of the situation, however. Today, almost all interventions with young people who are considered at high risk (of something bad, although it is not always clear of what) continue to demand compliance from them at all costs, frequently including through the use of force and violence. The state (the public) continues to endorse and actively support the violence associated with this compliance. In Canada, the state even provides particular methods of violent containment, considered legitimate, and actively trains youth workers in applying these methods. Almost all programs and services offered to youth-at-risk require that they comply with at least some pre-determined expectations; at a minimum, these include attendance, cooperation, completion of responsibilities and/or chores, etc. Perhaps more disturbingly, such expectations can typically also include the use of particular language conventions (such as manners) and the prohibition of other language conventions (such as swearing) as well as compliance with particular cultural and, in some cases, spiritual standards.

What even a casual survey of programs and services for youth reveals is that for virtually all of them, compliance is the core operative component and is rigorously enforced by the professionals who run the program or service. This is most obvious in programs and services that provide housing for young people, such as group homes, residential treatment programs, boarding schools and shelters for homeless youth. In all of these kinds of programs, compliance is enforced in relation to very specific rules and procedures that govern everything, from when it is time to wake up, to the precise sequence of morning routines, and what sorts of activities are appropriate to the kinds of foods that can be consumed. Such rules and procedures are almost always universally enforced for all of the children and youth residing in a particular program. These are group rules that are enforced as a mechanism of control.

Therefore, these kinds of rules and procedures are not usually customized or personalized to fit with the particular circumstances of individual children or youth.

The consequences for non-compliance are severe. On the surface, we might only think about those consequences that relate to the immediate context of the young person. A common consequence for failing to follow the procedures at bedtime, for example, is that the young person involved will have to go to bed earlier the following night. In some services, a common consequence for failing to follow the morning routines in a prescribed time frame is that the young person will miss breakfast and will have to wait until lunch for some food. These kinds of consequences can be challenging to absorb for young people, but on the whole they are the least of the young person's problems. The effect of these kinds of consequences are short term and ultimately undone with relative ease. The real consequence from non-compliance is much more harmful than these kinds of short term measures. Young people who fail to comply with the rules and procedures of a service or program may be excluded from such service or program altogether, with the professionals deciding that the young person "is not suited for the program". This is a common scenario for those young people in need of mental health treatment, admitted to residential treatment programs and then discharged shortly thereafter as a result of failing to comply with the rules of the program. These young people are said to be not ready for treatment. They have not yet made a commitment to the treatment process. Therefore, they are ineligible to receive mental health treatment services until they can demonstrate a greater level of compliance.

Ironically, the more often a young person fails to comply, the more intense the demands for compliance become. It is common practice, for example, to require young people who have been non-compliant with certain routines and procedures to sign a "contract" that lays out the compliance expectations for a prescribed time frame, including not only what sorts of expectations must be followed, but also how they must be followed. Such contracts are then vigorously monitored and the young person "on contract" is held to the highest standard of compliance imaginable (Gharabaghi, 2010).

What becomes apparent in this kind of process is that, from the perspective of the professionals, the young person is being recklessly non-compliant and must be motivated or forced to abandon such reckless behavior as quickly as possible. The young person's behavior, or non-compliance, is seen as willful and strategic; this is why the standards around expected compliance are continuously raised in the face of non-compliance so that the young person understands that this is a battle he or she will lose, either because the professionals will continue to raise the standards, or because they will discharge or abandon him or her altogether with some rationale for why this is the right thing to do. What is completely absent from this process is any sort of consideration for the possibility that the young person's non-compliance with a particular expectation makes sense from the perspective of the young person and is reflective of strength and resilience, rather than weakness and a problematic behavior. Alternatively, also dismissed is the possibility that the young person's non-compliance is not willful or reckless but rather symptomatic of deeply embedded mental health concerns, trauma or developmental challenges.

As it turns out, the need for compliance trumps all other considerations. Regardless of mental health issues, developmental challenges or even embedded trauma, young people must do as they are told, because what they are being told to do by professional care givers or interveners is in their best interest. As it turns out, there are striking similarities between the best interests of virtually unlimited numbers of young people, regardless of their unique identities, histories and personal stories. Their best interests, as it turns out, is to conform to the norm.

THE MYTH OF UNIQUENESS

In spite of a broad recognition among youth work professionals that each young person brings their own story; their own unique circumstances; and their own constellation of issues, problems, prospects and promises, it is enormously difficult to identify junctures in the everyday practice of youth work that confirm, support, nurture or promote such uniqueness. Fundamentally, youth work is driven by surprisingly orthodox assumptions about human development, criteria of success, indicators of personal growth and allowable approaches to social engagement. In everyday practice, youth work presents no alternative ways of understanding core issues or themes in young people's lives, including such complex themes as suicide, self harm, trauma, social negotiation, resistance, rebellion or entrepreneurial initiative. Much of the everyday practice of youth work professionals is predictably concerned with young people's behavior, social manners, academic accomplishment and psychological stability. The true measure of developmental health is not the expression of uniqueness, but the degree of conformity to broad social standards that have been adopted fully by youth work professionals and the systems within which they work.

Organizations and agencies providing services to edgy youth would seriously question this characterization of professional youth work and youth services. They would undoubtedly argue that they do indeed pay careful attention to the unique needs of every young person and that their services are tailored to meet such unique needs. They would point to their approach of developing treatment plans and the opportunities for young people to have a voice in this process as indicators of their commitment to individualize, personalize or customize their services. Most such organizations and agencies have elaborate value statements as well as policies and procedures to proactively respond to issues of diversity and multiple identities. Furthermore, most provide special training to their professional youth workers so that they may be aware of and competent enough to work with diversity and multiple identities. On paper, the systems and structures designed to respond to edgy youth are indeed responsive to the young people's uniqueness.

In practice, however, we see much of these rhetorical features of service structures and approaches disappear. As it turns out, virtually all services are informed by very similar and certainly overlapping theoretical premises, academic disciplines and organizational structures. These services respond to the same accountability and reporting requirements imposed typically by a handful of funders, mostly governmental. They exist within common legal frameworks related to human resource management, employment standards and health and safety regulation. They also draw on the same psychological frameworks, ranging from developmental psychology to cognitive behavioral therapeutic approaches to behaviorism.

The expectations imposed on professional youth workers are governed by common job descriptions, and consequences for under-performance, or performing outside of the framework laid out by superiors, are swift and uncompromising. Professional youth workers are hired to implement already existing programs and routines, not to bring their own exceptionalities to their relationships with young people. The workers know in advance what they will be asked to report to superiors and to other members of the multi-disciplinary team. Therefore, their efforts in being with edgy youth are geared toward observations that correspond to the categories of reporting. As it turns out, notwithstanding the informal appearance of professional youth work in the moment, this informality is substantially shaped and monitored by a rather formal and regulated approach to being with edgy youth.

Not surprisingly, it is difficult to imagine how young people can experience services and professional youth work interventions without feeling that their uniqueness is being attacked, or dismissed as peripheral to the process of intervention, at the very least. It becomes readily apparent that the bulk of the service system, and by extension, professional youth work, is already established in a particular way, and young people must find ways of fitting into these systems. This is very different from what the rhetoric of individualization, personalization and customization suggests; services, it turns out, do not reinvent themselves continuously to respond to the uniqueness of each young person. Instead, they expect young people to make the necessary adjustments in order to conform to the structural needs of service provision and professional intervention before any such service or intervention has actually been delivered. Quite legitimately, one might argue, faced with the demand for conformity right from the start, edgy youth dig in deep and construct their resistance with considerable skill, for better or for worse.

THE LOGIC OF RESISTANCE

Although it is always very frustrating when professionals encounter young people who just don't respond to professional interventions (even when these are evidence-based), it is not always clear who is more frustrated, the professional or the young person. For the professional, the frustration is based on the recognition that in spite of holding much power, having access to enormous resources (both material and knowledge-based resources) and even having been given a mandate for coercion if necessary, this still is no match for the simple act of resistance perpetrated by the young person. For the young person, however, the frustration is of a very different nature. For edgy youth, in particular, it is the frustration of being presented with lame and routine interventions that speak neither to the young person's specialness nor to his or her desire to explore, discover, risk, soar and crash. Edgy youth are concerned about the helping systems' inability to see beyond themselves, to recognize a world where patented, standardized, and packaged interventions simply don't work. Furthermore, edgy youth are concerned that their resistance to such lame interventions is misunderstood by most of the helping systems as well as by virtually all of the helping professionals.

The core of professional misunderstanding of the resistance on the part of edgy youth is the idea that the resistance presented by these young people must be overcome in order to move forward. Fundamentally, virtually all approaches to intervention with edgy youth aim to do just that: they aim to overcome resistance and introduce conformity. Resistance is articulated as a problem, a barrier to growth, a challenge in need of resolution. From the perspective of edgy youth, however, resistance is not a problem at all. To the contrary, edgy youth wear their resistance as a badge of honor, and what they really aim to achieve in their journey to adulthood is learning the skills necessary for greater resistance at more sophisticated levels and related to more complex and far-reaching issues and themes. These young people are not simply resisting a rule that is being imposed on them by a professional youth worker, or an expectation imposed by their school. They are resisting the very foundation of social conventions and expectations, and they are seeking to build their resistance into an alternative way of being: being within themselves and being with others.

The focus on resisting makes eminent sense from the perspective of edgy youth. They have learned, often through many experiences (some traumatic), that not much is to be gained from conformity. Unlike other young people, the payoff related to every day cooperation, collaboration and conformity has not been delivered. To the contrary, they have been led astray by false promises, shaky commitments, and outright abuse and violations. Nonetheless, it is not simply the repeated exposure to disappointment and deceit that has led edgy youth to find comfort in resistance. The results of these repeated experiences have been much more critical understanding and perspectives on human interaction, social relations, and cultural features of modern societies on the part of these young people. Edgy youth see things other young people cannot see. Edgy youth think about things that other young people dismiss as irrelevant. Moreover, edgy youth withhold their trust and even their presence when confronted with the everyday symptoms of blind conformity and uncritical acceptance of authority, rules and expectations.

Perhaps the most concise way of representing the resistance of edgy youth to helping systems and the professionals who work within these systems is in the form of a question: "Why should it be this way?" Edgy youth ask this question frequently and of everyone, including professional youth workers. Surprisingly, or perhaps predictably, few people can answer this question.

Perhaps we have grown accustomed to the idea that young people don't really need to know why things are the way they are. Perhaps because most young people never ask this question, or at least don't insist on an answer, we have become complacent toward ensuring that we can answer the question if we were to be asked. Or perhaps we, including those among us who make a living interacting with young people, simply don't know the answer. The reality for edgy youth is that this question is critical in everyday survival. Without challenging others about their intentions, their activities or their decisions, the risk of abuse, neglect, abandonment, rejection and dismissal increases significantly. Edgy youth have learned to judge the quality of help and guidance they encounter not by its content, but by how well it stands up to the question, "Why should it be this way?" Sometimes additional questions might be asked, including, "Why can it not be *that* way?" or, "Will you support me if I choose to try it that way?"

There are at least four good reasons for edgy youth to resist the expectations of professional helpers and helping systems. The four good reasons to resist are:

- The lack of personalization
- The evidence that there will not be benefits
- Questions about the integrity of the helper
- The mediocrity of the promised outcome

These are not reasons to dismiss or ignore those expectations, but simply to resist excessive compliance and immediate responsiveness, and instead to challenge such expectations in order to make sure that compliance and cooperation will eventually produce value to the youth. Edgy youth are, often to the annoyance of helpers, much too suspicious to accept the promise of a better future in exchange for immediate compliance at face value.

The Lack of Personalization

It is not lost on edgy youth that helpers and helping systems often claim to have solutions to their problems before they even meet the young person. The solutions offered are very obviously prefabricated and based largely on the prototype of a young person who meets certain diagnostic or social criteria. Expectations about the young person's conduct, everyday routines and expected accomplishments are laid out at the time of admission to a program or service; specific workers are assigned to the young person without his or her input; and goals and outcomes are articulated with the young person present, but without having created a context in which most young people would feel comfortable to speak their mind and to assert their perspectives. Edgy youth know that the language and friendly approaches associated with their interactions with helpers and helping systems does not mitigate the fact that they are ultimately assigned a client number, and given access to or have imposed upon them the same or a very similar service as the previous client. Given the sensation of being seen as a number, of being denied assistance that is personalized based on the young person's identity and specialness, it makes sense for that young person to resist such help. Resistance, in this instance, is simply a way of forcing the helper to get to know the young person and forcing the helping system either to adapt to the specialness of this young person or to come clean on its limitations, and to proceed with disassociating with the young person and making excuses for why help cannot be provided.

The Evidence that there will not be Benefits

It is most peculiar that helpers and helping systems often engage edgy youth as if those young people lived in a social vacuum and had no way of communicating with other edgy youth who have already received services. In fact, edgy youth are socially well connected and have their own networks of peers who provide references and stories about their experiences with particular helpers and helping systems. Unfortunately, many of the experiences shared, and stories told, are negative. Within their own peer networks, edgy youth find abundant evidence that the approaches taken by helpers and helping systems will not work. Virtually all edgy youth have friends and acquaintances who have already received extensive "help" from the professional sectors, and who now find themselves homeless and in despair. Many edgy youth have lost friends either to long term incarceration or to suicide. Edgy youth know that their journey of personal growth and development will not be as simple or straightforward as their helpers and their helping systems often pretend. They see the evidence of hardship, chronic failure and ultimately of being rejected even by the very helpers now professing to have their best interests at heart everywhere around them. In this context, it makes sense to resist the helpers and their helping systems, challenge them to work harder, have them prove their commitment to the young person's journey, even when that journey does not always take the path proposed by the helper.

Questions about the Integrity of the Helper

Edgy youth are far too wise to belief that an individual employed in the helping professions will necessarily perform his or her duties with integrity. They have learned (often the hard way) that just because one becomes a parent that does not mean that one will parent with love and nurturance. Just because one chooses policing as a career does not mean that one will uphold the law and live as a law abiding citizen. Furthermore, just because one chooses a helping profession as one's career does not mean that one is above abuse, or self-serving and egotistical behavior. From the perspective of edgy youth, helpers are best assumed to be corrupt and to pose a risk to young people, since naïve faith in their integrity can have miserable consequences, whereas helpers who demonstrate that they are not corrupt will work hard to convince the young person of their integrity and good intentions. As far as edgy youth are concerned, helpers who may not think of themselves as corrupt, but who reject the young people who resist them, lack the integrity required to be helpful to them. Indeed, the helper's response to a young person's resistance is ultimately an excellent measure of the helper's integrity.

The Mediocrity of Promised Outcomes

Living on the edge and taking on an edgy identity prepares young people for extremes; edgy youth don't do very well with mediocrity. Their dreams about the future are often extraordinary, their goals are lofty, and their preparedness to fight and challenge is great. For this reason, many edgy youth experience a major process of deflation while engaging with helpers and their helping systems. As it turns out, the outcomes encouraged by helpers and their helping systems are often profoundly unattractive to edgy youth. Furthermore, the process required to achieve such outcomes simply does not seem worth it. Much of what the professional helping sector has to offer is really quite banal. "If you follow the rules, study hard in school, and take your meds every day, you might find a job that will allow you to earn enough to pay for rent and food in a subsidized housing situation." These kinds of outcomes are hardly inspiring to edgy youth, having spent much of their lives living the extremes of absolute misery and astonishing highs. Once again, it makes eminent sense for edgy youth to resist the imposition of mediocrity and to challenge helpers and the helping systems to recognize them potentially as the leaders of tomorrow and as individuals with hopes for greatness and the capacity to achieve it.

There are many other reasons why it might make sense for edgy youth to resist professional helpers and their helping systems. In some cases, it is as simple as avoiding further abuse or trauma. In other cases, it may be more complex and related to the acknowledgment of a young person's specialness. Regardless of the trigger reason for resistance, edgy youth know that compliance and cooperation will result in services and approaches to being helped that are likely to be unsuccessful, however each edgy youth might define their "success". Perhaps surprisingly, professional helpers and their helping systems are poorly equipped to deal with such resistance on the part of edgy youth. Instead of allowing the youth to embark on a path that works for them and providing assistance and guidance along that path, many professional helpers and their helping systems are resistant to young people making choices and taking initiative. As a result, they respond to the resistance offered up by the edgy youth with increased efforts to break through it. Far from being encouraged to stop and reflect, professional helpers often intensify their use of persuasion and coercion, finding ways to rationalize this within the obscurity of clinical evidence and psycho-babble.

THE LIMITATIONS OF PERSUASION AND COERCION

Professional helpers and their helping systems are much less concerned about the edgy youth on their case loads than they are about what edgy youth do on a day-to-day basis. This may be a subtle distinction, but it is an important one. In effect, it points to the profound dialectics of helper-youth dyads and their experiences together. Whereas young people seek to develop themselves, enrich their experiences, strive toward their often fantastic goals and dreams, and feel like they are becoming somebody, helpers are concerned with the everyday indicators of the quality of decision-making on the part of the youth, their progress toward articulated goals, their capacity to avoid trouble, and the extent of their cooperation with the service plans written into their case files and reviewed regularly for progress made. Helpers observe, analyze and respond to the actions of edgy youth. As part of their responses, helpers seek to convince youth to abandon habits that do not fit with their existing service plans and adopt habits that support that plan instead. In so doing, helpers use two related, but unique approaches: they seek to persuade and coerce young people into compliance.

Most professional helpers working with edgy youth are good people with good intentions. They want young people to succeed. Challenges emerge when helpers want young people to succeed all the time, in an incremental fashion with a steady trend toward greater and greater accomplishments. Professional helpers are generally not too happy when young people deviate from the master plan pursuant to the path to success. In order to avoid such deviation, the helpers employ the same strategies we might find in politics, advertising, and international trade negotiations; they seek to persuade the young person to see the world their way. The goal of the helper is to convince the young person that acting according to the "plan" is in their best interest. Indeed, acting in any way that violates or deviates from that plan is not rational, symptomatic of the young person's problems and is in immediate need of correction. In support of this approach to persuasion, professional helpers employ many different strategies and tools, including role modeling, logic, values and a full spectrum of coercive techniques.

Role Modeling

Professional helpers seek to demonstrate good decision-making, thoughtful action, discipline and social competence in their everyday work with edgy youth. In institutional settings, such role modeling can simply consist of being at work on time and dressed appropriately as well as working collaboratively with colleagues. In community-based settings, such role modeling may require a more open approach to boundaries so that the young person can get a glimpse of the "successful" life of the helper. It is often frustrating to professional helpers when edgy youth fail to appreciate the role modeling presented by the helper and the lessons contained within it. The message to the young person is, "If I can do it, you should also be able to do it."

As it turns out, edgy youth often do not respond as expected to such role modeling. This is not entirely surprising since the life context of edgy youth differs substantially from that of the professional helper. Yet somehow such differences are often overlooked, and helpers expect edgy youth to adjust their conduct to match that of the helper. Role modeling is of limited use when it precisely accentuates those differences between youth and practitioner that reflect the social disadvantage faced by the young person. An additional limitation of role modeling is its emphasis on a single path to success. Partly because of the unique context of edgy youth, but also corresponding to the developmental norm, young people are highly reactive to being asked to follow a path that has been laid out by someone else. Finding one's own path is part of the journey of growing up, and edgy youth are, quite rightly so, reticent in giving up this "right".

Logic

It often seems that using logic as a tool of persuasion is value-neutral and simply conveys the facts of life in a reasonable and meaningful manner. Professional helpers often seek to help young people make sense of their lives, decisions and conduct. They convey messages such as, "It doesn't make sense to act out right now," or, "If you do the work now, you won't have to do it later." Professional helpers convey a sense of adamancy about being logical in one's approach to life, and about fighting against all things for which a rational foundation cannot be found. In this way, edgy youth are expected to be reflective, think ahead, weigh the possible consequences of their decisions and actions, and deny themselves uncertainty and risk on an everyday basis.

The insistence on the use logic imposed on young people is really another way of holding young people to a standard of thought and action that reflects an ideal model few people, including few professional helpers, can maintain or even ever achieve. In reality, very little of everyday life is based on logic. Relationships, intimacy, love, risk, exploration and many other meaningful and developmentally appropriate processes are forms of resisting logic every day and in the moment. Demanding that young people forgo such illogical processes, in favor of responding robotically to their social context, is tantamount to asking them to abandon their identity. Once again, edgy youth react to such demands. They typically have very little left to hold on to, but certainly their developing identity is one personal possession edgy youth are unlikely to give up, even in the name of logic.

Values

Where the supposed value-neutrality of logic fails, professional helpers employ another tool of persuasion, other than logic, that attacks young people from the opposite direction. This is the repertoire of values that are said to be pro-social and the building blocks of a worthy and respected human being. Professional helpers are not always conscious of just how much they seek to influence the value systems of young people; they utilize language and concepts that appear, on the surface, to be unquestionably positive and useful.

Thus, the imposition of these values appears unproblematic. Common values that are propagated by professional helpers include the values of sharing, cooperation, honesty, discipline and a strong work ethic. In some cases, values may also include spiritual dimensions based on the faith foundation of a particular helper or helping organization.

It is not inherently problematic that values find their way into the persuasion strategies of professional helpers. Values are indeed foundational elements of identity and whatever path one might choose to personal development and growth. The difficulty with reflecting such surface values in one's persuasion strategy is that this often either clashes with or contradicts the afore-mentioned role modeling. In fact, edgy youth are sufficiently observant to notice the lack of sharing and cooperation, and often the nuances of dishonesty in the conduct of their professional helpers. In institutional settings, such as residential care settings, schools, custody facilities and hospitals, edgy youth have too often experienced a lack of commitment to hard work and professional discipline on the part of the very helpers and helping organizations propagating such values. As much as edgy youth reject simple, expectation-laden approaches to role modeling, they resent hypocrisy and contradictions in the conduct of professional helpers and the organization they work for even more.

The Spectrum of Coercive Techniques

If one could visually represent the proportion of the use of coercion as the driving element in the persuasion efforts of professional helpers, most observers would be very surprised at just how extensive the use of coercive techniques really is. Perhaps this is the result of insufficient time spent reflecting on one's work, or perhaps it is due to low quality supervision and feedback. The reality is that much of the professional help offered to edgy youth relies heavily on coercive elements. It is important to recognize that such coercive elements represent a wide range of coercive techniques that are nuanced and often difficult to recognize on one end of the spectrum, while on the other end of the spectrum they are quite clearly violent and, at times, brutal. More nuanced uses of coercive techniques include the implying of consequences that are designed to make the young person uncomfortable, anxious or exploit his or her vulnerabilities. This might include quite nuanced threats to withdraw fun opportunities or privileges: "You really need to do your chore since otherwise I am not sure we will be able to go to the movies."

It might also aim more directly at the young person's vulnerabilities: "Do this or I will cancel your family visit this weekend." Within the spectrum of coercive techniques, professional helpers employ threats of consequences, actually impose consequences, withdraw opportunities and privileges, withhold love and nurture, and deny rights to privacy and social engagement. Ultimately, at the extreme end of coercion, they physically contain young people in confined spaces; wrestle young people to the ground and hold them there; or in some situations, even chemically subdue young people through injections and rapid-acting medications (Internations' Justice Federation, nd).

The spectrum of coercive techniques is not meant to be damaging to young people. Even the most grotesque forms of coercion are assumed to be helpful and legitimate interventions that will ultimately assist young people in adopting "the right sort of conduct". Such interventions are usually rationalized in terms of maintaining safety for the young person affected as well as others potentially impacted by the conduct of the young person. Alternatively, they are rationalized as necessary "corrective interventions" to accelerate the young person's resignation and acceptance of the imposed path. Edgy youth rarely accept this sort of persuasion. These young people are very experienced in all matters concerning violence and they have a deep understanding of the nuances of violence and the profound negation of virtue and values that the violence represents. As a result, while edgy youth can be temporarily subdued through the use of the coercive techniques of persuasion, they cannot be changed in this way. To the contrary, edgy youth will respond to violence in kind; they often do so just when the professional helpers and their professional systems are about to celebrate their competence and brilliance. This is when the helping systems involved with edgy youth perpetrate the ultimate act of persuasion, directed no longer at the young people but instead at their funders and the public at large: "This young person cannot be helped." "He is untreatable." "She needs long term containment, secure treatment or incarceration."

Professional helpers and their helping systems have encountered the limits of persuasion and coercive techniques very frequently; the outcomes of helping services in their engagement with edgy youth are universally unimpressive. Helping systems have learned to shift their persuasion efforts from young people who refused to be persuaded to their funders and the public. One of the common elements associated with the failure of persuasion in the engagement of edgy youth is the omission of focus on actually getting to know each edgy youth as a distinct, unique and worthy individual. Doing so requires a very particular skill that increasingly has gone by the wayside in the helping professions; this is the skill of being with edgy youth.

STARTING AGAIN

The first step toward a radically different way of engaging edgy youth is to let go of the enormous arrogance of most professional practices within the youth-serving sectors. The second step is to stop making this work strictly about ourselves: our needs, our desires, our expectations and our values. Finally, the third step is to find the capacity, deep within us, to value and respect the specialness of edgy youth. These three steps really need to be practiced and then taken well before we encounter any edgy youth. These steps are the starting point for a meaningful engagement, a foundation for respectful relationships and the conduit for mutual caring and guidance between helper and young person.

Letting Go of Professional Arrogance

We cannot let go of our professional arrogance unless we acknowledge that it is ever-present. We started this chapter by pointing out that membership in the youth-serving professions does not, in and of itself, imply competence, virtue or any sort of special commitment to young people. The capacity to use language that reflects higher levels of education in fields, such as child and youth care, social work, or more academic disciplines such as psychology or sociology in no way represents evidence of competence. Such pre-service educational preparation may provide stronger foundations for a career in the helping professions, but much work needs to be done every day to translate one's conceptual and theoretical understanding into meaningful practices and ways of engaging edgy youth. High marks on a dozen psychology courses do not, in any shape or form, constitute proof of the ability to understand a particular edgy youth. The only way of getting to know a young person is to be with that young person in his or her life space[2]. This takes time and requires

---

[2] A more extensive discussion of the concept of life-space can be found in chapter 5; for now, suffice it to say that this concept has traditionally referred to being with and working with young people where their lives unfold; it is seen as an alternative to office-based counseling and therapy interventions. Much of the discussion about life space in this book is based on Gharabaghi & Stuart, 2012.

that one does less and observes more; speaks less and listens more; and impose oneself less onto the young person and, instead, allow the young person to discover a path that is interesting and meaningful to him or her.

It's Not about You

It is unfortunate that much of social work training, similar to child and youth care training, identifies the worker as the agent of change. According to the textbooks, the worker is very important in the development and growth of the young person. This is partly true, but it is also very misleading. The worker is indeed important as one party to the relationship. However, the worker is not so important that the other party to the relationship, the edgy youth, becomes incidental, peripheral, and acknowledged mostly in his or her responses to the worker. Ultimately, it is not just about who is important, but also about who gets to set the agenda, the tone, the goals and the values within the relationship. We must learn to be with edgy youth in order to gain insight into their expectations of the present and the future; the values with which they wish to build their foundation of development and growth; and, ultimately, the path they wish to explore, for better or for worse. We might think we know best and, indeed, we might be able to help young people avoid unnecessary detours into dead ends and failures. In the end, however, edgy youth will not accept a path as unworthy or reflective of poor choices unless they have actually travelled it. More often than not, being with edgy youth means that we travel with them on their path.

Valuing and Respecting Edgy Youth

We all claim to value and respect edgy youth, but this is entirely irrelevant if we are not authentic and honest in this claim. Many helping professionals are unable to respond to simple questions such as, "What precisely do you value about this edgy young person?" or, "What do you respect about that edgy young person?" It is likely that most helping professionals have a general respect for the concept of edgy youth, but not necessarily for any particular edgy young person who is not meeting their expectations and who fails to respond to their efforts to change him or her into a productive and conformist citizen. In fact, the need to value and respect edgy youth in such a way that they can recognize that they are being valued and respected, not just as a conceptual demographic but as many different individuals, challenges the helpers and their helping systems in a very big way. Yet, this is where we must pause for a moment and reflect deeply on our work with edgy youth. If we cannot even find an authentic and honest sense of respect for these young people within ourselves, how can we possibly think that our fancy approaches, evidence-based interventions and well-researched ideas will make any difference to those youth who will not comply or conform?

This is the question we will turn to in the next chapter. In order to move forward, we need to really think about what edgy youth can offer us as professional helpers and communities and societies at large.

Chapter 3

DON'T TAKE IT PERSONALLY

It is amazing how we can spend years knowing that we are ignoring the plight of edgy youth, turning a blind eye toward their neglect and abandonment and pretending that we cannot notice them loitering on the streets and/or in the coffee shops, and then very quickly become offended and perhaps even indignant when they in-turn ignore our sudden interest in them after they are referred to our programs and services. Whether we are involved with edgy youth as social workers, counselors or child and youth care professionals who spend each and every day with them in the context of institutional- or community-based care, we are masters at making our presence in their lives fundamentally about ourselves. Although all professional helpers are taught in their pre-service training not to personalize the behaviors of young people, particularly their offensive behaviors, it turns out that it is surprisingly difficult to remember that this work is not really about us.

In this chapter, I want to explore why it appears to be so difficult to avoid personalizing the things that edgy youth do either to us or in spite of us. I also want to distinguish between different modes of personalizing. After all, there is something virtuous about becoming personally involved with edgy youth. Far from being necessarily the wrong thing to do, or an indication of problems, it may also signal a higher level commitment to edgy youth than one might find with helpers who seem to not be impacted at all by the actions (or inactions) of the young people. What does seem to be clear, however, is that we must really reflect at a much deeper level about the reasons for personalizing, the purposes of doing so, and its consequences. We also must reflect on the possible perspectives of young people with respect to personalizing within helper-young person interactions. As is so often the case, the perspective of edgy youth on elements associated with their relationships and interactions with helpers is informed by a different set of values, beliefs, experiences and expectations than that of adults, helpers or society at large. Without exploring how young people, and especially edgy youth, think about and experience responses to them on the part of helpers and other adults in society, and without at least hypothesizing about their intentions and motivations, we might be missing significant information and limit our understanding of what is going on in our relationships with them. In this chapter I aim to explore, in detail, the issue of personalizing on the part of helpers as well as the experience of such personalizing from the perspective of edgy youth. My hope is that this exploration will lead us to the starting point of thinking differently about being with edgy youth and opening new opportunities for our mutual engagement.

THE REASONS FOR PERSONALIZING

It is important to be clear about what I mean by "personalizing". The concept of personalizing is often taken as synonymous to the process of taking it personally. This, however, misses several important nuances of the concept. To take things personally means that we assume generalized statements (typically offensive statements) to be specifically about us. Thus, when a young person uses profanity to vent and perhaps directs particular insults toward us, we assume that the young person is angry with us and we are unhappy or indignant about this. We take personally what the young person expressed as a general statement of frustration or unhappiness. Taking things personally is naturally a problem when working with edgy youth who typically experience very high levels of frustration and disappointment in everyday life. As professional helpers, we must maintain sufficient perspective as well as skill to distinguish generalized expressions of frustration and disappointment versus specific challenges to us, reflecting particular tensions in the interpersonal relationships between ourselves and the edgy youth. This is a topic which we will discuss in some detail later in this chapter. For now, however, it is important to distinguish between taking something personally and personalizing it. When we personalize things, we are doing much more than simply assuming that a statement was directed at us, and we feel much more complex emotions than simply feeling insulted and indignant. Personalizing means that we assume our Self, our presence and our very existence to be of central importance in a particular dynamic, process or interaction. Whatever the context of personalizing might be, we take ownership over that context, and we negate, in that process, the presence and ownership of the other person or group of people.

A personalizing response is much more common than we are typically willing to acknowledge. It turns out that it is quite challenging to allow another person to express their perspective on a particular issue in such a way that their presence and their Self is at the center of the story without immediately trying to find a place (often a central place) for ourselves in that story. For most of us, including those of us with extensive training in the helping professions, putting aside ourselves in order to allow someone else's experience to take center stage is difficult. Furthermore, when that other person is an edgy youth who tells stories that frequently challenge our sensibilities, our sense of right and wrong and our sense of safety, it is all the more tempting to intervene in that story by inserting ourselves as central characters or even by taking ownership over the story and making it our own. This personalizing is problematic in the helping professions, even more so than taking things personally because this form of personalizing is not always obvious. Once discovered or exposed, however, it can result in significant trust issues and relationship challenges.

This still leaves us with the question of why professional helpers might personalize their experiences with edgy youth when they ought to know about the potentially destructive and certainly unconstructive implications of doing so. We can identify at least three reasons for this. First, we have to consider the possibility that some professional helpers simply cannot relate to the experiences of edgy youth at all. Therefore, in order to find common ground with the youth, they work hard to recast their stories into ones that involve them in central and also in more familiar ways. This reason for personalizing is not intended to be offensive or oppressive; quite to the contrary, it is intended to create bridges and points of connection between helper and young person. From the helper's perspective, personalizing the stories of young people provides opportunities for reinventing those stories on familiar and, therefore, comfortable grounds. For most helpers, the oppressive aspects associated with this reason for personalizing are invisible. From the perspective of young people, on the other hand, helpers who personalize the young person's story are, in effect, hijacking that story and taking ownership over something that is clearly not theirs. The rejection expressed by young people in response to this reason for personalizing then takes on a life of its own, and the helper rejected in this way quickly moves from personalizing the young person's story to taking the young person's rejection personally. What started as a well-meant approach to finding connections with young people, quickly turns into a negative and escalating process of building and reinforcing indignation and rejection, both on the part of the helper and young person.

A second reason for personalizing reflects the often unspoken tension between helpers and edgy youth, and the wide gulf that exists between living at the center and living on the edge. For many helpers, there is nothing worth engaging with on the edges of the plateau, and the goal of connecting with edgy youth is to pull them off the edge and into the center. Personalizing in this context involves negating the identity and everyday experiences of edgy youth and instead imposing one's own. This is a much more explicitly malignant reason for personalizing, involving a judgment and rejection of the values and identities of edgy youth. Helpers who personalize for this reason often lack the imagination to think beyond their own experiences, and they certainly lack the preparedness to consider the values and possibilities embedded in other ways of experiencing everyday life. This reason for personalizing has many important implications, including how young people might over-compensate in their response to be being rejected, and also in terms of how outcomes and the performance of helpers and helping systems are measured. When there is an *a priori* rejection of the everyday context of edgy youth, what is really being measured, in terms of intervention outcomes, is the degree to which these young people begin to comply and ultimately conform to whatever values and expectations are imposed by the helper and the helping system.

From the perspective of young people, this reason for personalizing on the part of the helper calls for a strong and adamant response. Many edgy youth over-compensate in their responses to helpers who reject their everyday experiences as wrong, lacking value or meaning. Far from opening channels for mutual understanding and on-going dialogue, these youth ensure that the gulf between helper and young person widens and that the opportunities to explore strengths and vulnerabilities together in many different approaches to the everyday are largely destroyed. In many service settings, the youth simply leave when helpers personalize their work with edgy youth for this reason. For decades in residential care, the concept of "going Awol", or of leaving the institution without permission, has served as the symbol of the edgy youth's rejection after having their approach to the everyday dismissed. Therefore, in this context, personalizing is less about "taking things personally" and more about re-casting the everyday experiences of edgy youth in such a way that they are centered around the personal values and assumptions of the helpers and the helping systems.

A third mode of personalizing is closely tied into the power dynamics of helper-youth relationships. In this mode of personalizing, helpers seek to prioritize their own needs over those of the young person. This is often masked by a declaratory commitment to assist young people in meeting goals and conforming to treatment or intervention plans. Ultimately, however, it is a mode of personalizing in which the helper seeks to ensure that his or her needs for control, choice, decision-making authority, self-esteem and prestige are met. For many helpers in the youth serving professions, the power and authority associated with "caring for" or "watching over" young people is a new experience, making them feel good and providing opportunities for new ways to experience oneself. Particularly in service settings where there is considerable emphasis on control, structure, routines and rules, the everyday routine of imposing authority can quickly become a core element of the helper's professional identity.

This particular mode of personalizing is in part driven by the challenges associated with connecting with edgy youth. In reality, most helpers experience many setbacks in their attempts to do so, and edgy youth often work hard to expose the vulnerabilities and the skill deficits of helpers. In an atmosphere where control is highly valued, helpers are reluctant to expose their vulnerabilities and often do whatever is necessary to impose their authority on edgy youth in order to ensure they are seen by colleagues and employers as competent and strong. Resistance on the part of youth is seen as a major threat to the helpers. Therefore, efforts are made to crush such resistance quickly and resolutely (Gharabaghi & Phelan, 2011).

From the perspective of young people, this reason for personalizing on the part of helpers is particularly difficult to reconcile with the declaratory commitments made by helpers and their helping systems from when they were first admitted to the particular program or service. It is often very clear and obvious that particular interventions or consequences imposed on young people have little to do with the needs of that young person and are instead about cementing the strength and authority of the helper involved. In particular, edgy youth are already suspicious about the integrity of the helping commitments made by professional helpers and their helping systems, given that much of these are representative of the core values and expectations of the center. However, edgy youth are well aware of the impact of organizational and system cultures on individual helpers and they understand that individual helpers are often driven less by their own values and expectations, and more by the real or perceived requirements of their employers and the judgment of their colleagues and peers. Indeed, in high structure settings that value control and compliance, helpers are subject to the control culture just as much as edgy youth. The need to maintain a high level of prestige based on the demonstrated capacity of imposing one's authority becomes a matter of personal safety. Edgy youth are experienced and skilled observers of professional helpers trying to balance the expectations of their colleagues and employers on the one hand, and their personal values and preferences for being with edgy youth on the other. An exclusive orientation toward meeting the expectations of colleagues and systems minimizes the role of the helper-youth relationship and tends to turn edgy youth away from those helpers; ignoring the expectations of colleagues and systems raises suspicion that the relationship between helper and youth may not be realistic or sustainable.

So far, we have explored three different reasons for personalizing on the part of the helper within the helper-youth relationship. It is not difficult to understand the origins of each of these reasons, and certainly all three present rational, or at least not baseless, responses to real issues and dilemmas faced by professional helpers in their work with youth. Each of these reasons for personalizing, however, also presents some significant problems and limitations in terms of maximizing the opportunities of helper-youth relationships. As we proceed to discuss personalizing in this chapter, we will now move toward a more positive and constructive discussion of the purposes of personalizing and how we might achieve the same goals without personalizing, or at least with a more reflective approach to personalizing in our everyday work with youth.

THE PURPOSES OF PERSONALIZING

Above we discussed some of the reasons why professional helpers might personalize issues and themes in their work with edgy youth, but we did not really explore what these professional helpers are trying to achieve by personalizing. In other words, what is the purpose of personalizing in helper-youth relationships?

I want to propose that there are three very distinct frameworks for understanding personalization in the helper-youth relationship, each tied around a personal characteristic that presents challenges to being with edgy youth. The three personal characteristics that are at the core of each of the three frameworks are fearfulness, self-doubt and narcissism. The first two of these provide opportunities for change that will enhance the helper's capacity to be with edgy youth; the third presents a core problem that can lead to major difficulties for edgy youth and also potentially impact on the good work of other helpers and systems. I will explore each of the frameworks for understanding the purpose of personalizing below.

Fearfulness

Most helpers are not different than anyone else; thus, they are fearful of the unfamiliar. By unfamiliar I mean all those things over which we cannot exert control. This includes the behavior of others, situations where the outcomes of our actions are not easily predicted, and relationships that lack some of the obvious foundations of familial connection, love, mutual respect, natural attraction, sexual stimulation or any of the other familiar reasons for coming together in relationship. Working with edgy youth is difficult, even at the best of times. One never quite knows what will happen next and edgy youth are notoriously negligent in communicating their intentions, interests, likes and dislikes, or anything about them that might help the helper gain confidence in his or her knowledge of what will happen next. On most days, being with edgy youth involves the presence of a hint of violence, often manifested by explicit or more nuanced verbal threats, and also by the physical tension evident in the body language of the young people. Under these circumstances, it is not surprising that helpers carry a considerable fear as they execute their day-to-day duties and try their best to engage with the youth.

Fear tends to make us protective about ourselves and our well-being. As a result of being fearful, we often take measures that place us in close proximity to the exit, to additional safety-related resources, and to maintain vigilance in our observations and supervision of the immediate physical and social context in which we find ourselves. In other words, when we are fearful, we tend to interpret whatever happens around us as potential threats to our safety. Therefore, we are always ready to respond in a protective and sometimes pre-emptive manner. We specifically personalize our surroundings in order to ensure that we are ready and able to respond when we believe ourselves to be in danger. Personalizing within this framework serves the purpose of ensuring our safety and well-being. We personalize things in order to mitigate our fearfulness and to move forward with whatever is demanded of us while working with edgy youth.

It is important to recognize that personalizing does not overcome our fearfulness; instead, it equips us to manage in spite of this fearfulness. By presuming that our safety and well-being are compromised because of the hint (or more overt presence) of violence among edgy youth, as well as because of the lack of predictability and the lack of familiar foundation for our relationship with the edgy youth, we personalize our presence with the edgy youth and maintain ourselves at the center of virtually everything that happens. We need to be at the center in order to not miss anything that might transition our compromised safety and well-being into real violations and transgressions.

Within this framework, personalizing achieves its purpose of mitigating our fearfulness by enforcing a sense of greater safety and well-being through mechanisms of greater vigilance and pre-emptive responses to perceived threats. This approach does not, however, help to open up opportunities for being with edgy youth differently, without the fearfulness and with possibilities of much deeper and profound connections. In order to create those opportunities, we must find ways not of mitigating our fearfulness but of overcoming it altogether. In other words, we must find ways of achieving the same purpose that this framework, based on fearfulness, seeks to achieve without centering it on fearfulness and the resulting personalizing.

One way of doing this is to complete the equation of helper-youth relationships. Much of the personalizing embedded in the process of mitigating fearfulness is based on only one side of this equation and does not take into account what might be happening for the young person on the other side of the equation. Could it be that this edgy youth, or even group of edgy youth, also experience fearfulness and take measures to mitigate this experience? Might there be an opportunity to come clean on both sides of the relationship and cancel out the need for fearfulness? In reality, edgy youth are afraid most of the time, not unlike the helpers assigned to assist them in their everyday tasks and activities. Also, edgy youth cannot predict what will happen next in their lives, and given the enormous power differential between young people on the edge and the helping systems based in the center, edgy youth have good reason to be suspicious and afraid of the possible consequences of engaging with helpers who represent that system of the center, after all. Moreover, as much as the helping system would like it to be different, edgy youth experience a hint, too, and sometimes much more than a hint, of violence in their interactions with helpers and their systems. At every level of interaction, edgy youth quite rationally equal the fearfulness of the helpers in their lives, and the relationships between themselves and their helpers take on a macabre dance of pretending it to be otherwise.

Within this framework, we recognize that personalizing is neither unique nor exclusive to the professional helpers. Indeed, edgy youth also personalize their experiences of the professional helpers and their helping systems, and they look to ensure that, as the everyday dynamics of a service setting unfold, they maintain proximity to the exit and an ability to respond quickly and decisively should they identify a serious threat to their safety and well-being. The net result in the dynamics of the helper-youth relationship is that both parties to the relationship are preoccupied with securing their personal safety and well-being, and both work hard to ensure the integrity of their separate safety systems. We have learned in many different contexts of social interaction that fearfulness embedded on both sides of a relationship begets increasingly greater protective actions that eventually produce frameworks for coexistence, rather than engagement. At a global level, we are reminded of the Cold War, during which fearfulness on the part of the two superpowers produced the intuitively insane doctrine of MAD (Mutually Assured Destruction), whereby each superpower produced sufficient military capacity to completely destroy the other. In the context of managing edgy youth in our societies, we have learned that incarcerating these young people in order to address the fears of communities and neighborhoods only serves to produce edgy adults on a mission to do harm and provide payback. Fear, we know, is a poor conduit for being together. It is absolutely necessary to overcome such fear on both sides of the equation and move on with the task of being together without building an armada of protective measures.

The fearfulness that drives the personalizing, embedded within the helper-youth relationship, can be addressed with a shift from separate protective measures to one joined protective measure that maintains safety and well-being. Rather than personalizing issues and themes that come up in being together with one another, both helper and young person can recast such issues and themes as relationship issues. The task is not to secure each party to the relationship, but rather the relationship itself. Therefore, the focus on engagement and interaction between helper and youth shifts from the entrenchment of individualized positions to the integration of concerns and challenges within the relationship; this also leads to a joint responsibility to produce solutions to such concerns and challenges.[1]

This framework for understanding personalization on the part of professional helpers exposes some of the deeply embedded assumptions we make about being with edgy youth. Far from accepting such "being with" as an equal partnership, we assume that it is of paramount importance to prepare ourselves, as professional helpers, to a degree of completion that leaves little

---

[1] This is the basis of what Garfat has referred to as *relational* child and youth care practice, whereby the focus of both the practitioner and the young person is on the relationship, as a space between the Self of the practitioner and the Self of the young person (Garfat, 2008).

room for partnership with the young people. A more reflective and democratic approach would consider the perspective of edgy youth in this context, possibly helping us to recognize that the fearfulness we experience as professional helpers is not caused by the edgy youth, but rather is a function of an inherently unfamiliar relationship. In this way, there is a shared fearfulness that can only be overcome in a partnership between its parties. This process is, in fact, a relationship-strengthening process that will produce benefits beyond the abandonment of personalizing, both on the part of the professional helper and the edgy youth.

Self-Doubt

For many professional helpers, the purpose of personalizing is driven not so much by the need to overcome fearfulness as it is by the need to manage a festering sense of self-doubt. Professional helpers who personalize their experiences within their relationships with edgy youth in order to overcome self-doubt are often confident about knowing what to do, but less confident about believing that they can actually do it. These helpers are well intentioned and committed to being in partnership with edgy youth, but frequently find themselves in positions of uncertainty and hesitate to follow through on their intentions to be with edgy youth without maintaining a protective shield of personalizing. They personalize specifically to overcome any doubt about what they are doing and they find certainty in their return in doing so from their attempts to abstain from personalizing.

The need to overcome self-doubt is often driven by the assumption that helping relationships require one party to be the knowing helper and another party to be the one being helped. In other words, many professional helpers fight their feelings of self-doubt simply because they assume, or frequently have been taught to believe, that self-doubt is a problem in helping relationships. Within this construction of helping relationships, partnership is dismissed once again, in favor of expertise and authority being centered around the helper. As a result, a great deal of pressure is placed on the helper to be able to control the relationship, both in terms of its activities and its experiences. This can only be done through the process of personalizing, so that what the helper is really controlling is not the relationship but his or her experience of the relationship as well as the activities of the young person within the relationship directed through mechanisms of control. Through the process of personalizing, the helper is able to remove any self-doubts since his or her actions are now responses to experiences over which he or she has full control.

This framework for understanding personalizing, in the context of the helper seeking to overcome self-doubt, helps to illuminate entirely new possibilities if we change the starting assumption. What if self-doubt is a positive element in relationships? What if the vulnerabilities created through self-doubt can be shared between helper and youth, and managing these vulnerabilities over time can become a joined project of the relationship, rather than the discreet responsibility of the helper? Once again, we find reason to pursue these possibilities further if we consider the perspective of the edgy youth in relation to self-doubt. Given their experiences with chronic mishaps, failure and things just not going their way, there is good reason to believe that edgy youth, too, are impacted by considerable self-doubt in their everyday experiences with helper-young person relationships. They typically know what to do and what to expect, but they often lack the ability to actually do things, to accomplish tasks and to produce the necessary outcomes. Edgy youth know that there are few external expectations for them to succeed, and low expectations breed low performance which, in turn, feeds the on-going self-doubt experienced by so many edgy youth.

As was the case in relation to fearfulness, self-doubt is also a characteristic that professional helpers often share with the young people they seek to help. Therefore, the opportunity presents itself once again to move forward together and to focus on the self-doubt embedded within the relationship, rather than the self-doubt carried by both parties to the relationship. Rather than overcoming self-doubt by personalizing the issues and themes encountered within the relationship, an alternative approach would suggest that this is something the relationship can take on as one of its characteristics, and the parties to the relationship can share the responsibilities associated with managing this self-doubt effectively, mitigating its impact. All that is required is for both parties to come to the realization that it is perfectly fine for a relationship to be uncertain about what it can do and where it might lead. It is also acceptable for parties in the relationship to take missteps, so long as these are co-owned and the responsibility of managing the consequences of such missteps is shared. Once again, we can achieve the purpose of personalizing without the process of personalizing; we can mitigate the impact of self-doubt without personalizing by moving in the opposite direction of partnership and by taking co-ownership of self-doubt in the context of the relationship.

It is becoming increasingly clear that, most of the time, the purpose of personalizing is not problematic or malignant; instead, it is a response to an overwhelming feeling of vulnerability on the part of the professional helper that, in most cases, finds a parallel dynamic among edgy youth as well. Re-thinking the core assumptions of being together, and in particular the belief that professional helpers must bring solutions and already sorted out pathways to success to edgy youth, results in opportunities to mitigate the consequences of vulnerability by simply shifting the focus of being together in the relationship, rather than on the two separate parties of the relationship. In this sense, personalizing does not need to be seen as a catastrophe or as the absolute corruption of being with edgy youth; instead, it may well be a reasonable starting point for the professional helper and the edgy youth involved to get started on a process of coming together within the relationship, and of fundamentally experiencing being together in a different manner. There is, however, a third framework for understanding the purpose of personalizing that takes on an entirely different direction and where the opportunities to enhance the experience of being together may be limited if not non-existent. This framework is supported by an entrenched narcissism on the part of the professional helper. This is what I will explore next.

Narcissism

For most professional helpers, a trusted and competent supervisor, mentor or peer is really all that is needed to ensure that the issue of personalizing does not become the sole purpose of being with edgy youth. Getting stuck as a result of either taking something personal or personalizing is very common in the youth serving professions. Getting unstuck is typically also achieved with relative ease, however, so long as someone is there to assist with perspective and guidance.[2] For some professional helpers, however, the issue of personalizing runs much deeper than that; they are affected by narcissism, and being advised to "get over it" or "not to take it personally" means nothing at all to them. They cannot help but personalize whatever it is they are experiencing, and when we really look carefully at their approach to being with edgy youth, we begin to see that, for these professional helpers, the work is really all about themselves.

Narcissism is often defined simply as having an inflated sense of one's own importance. One might think of terms such as egotistical or selfish as

---

[2] This is why scholars in child and youth care practice insist that supervision be considered an essential component of being with young people. See for example Magnuson & Burger (2001) as well as Cearley (2004).

meaning similar things. Narcissism has another element, however, that is especially relevant in the context of a framework for understanding the purpose of personalizing. Professional helpers affected by narcissism are unable to understand the world outside of their own experiences and, therefore, work very hard to recast all interaction with and engagement by others or of others to be fundamentally about themselves. They love to tell stories about themselves and include minute details that are not likely of interest to anyone else. They provide excessive information about their own relationships with others, and focus exclusively on their perception and experience of these relationships within these descriptions. They cannot sit idle and listen to someone else's stories without interrupting and forcibly changing the conversation to reflect stories about their own experiences once again.

These traits and compulsions present some very serious challenges to being with edgy youth. As we will discuss later in detail, being with edgy youth requires, first and foremost, respect for the presence of the other. To this end, it is very important that helpers are able to confirm the autonomy of the young person's experience and reflect a genuine and authentic interest in that experience. Professional helpers affected by narcissism are unable to do this and, in fact, frequently work hard to avoid doing this at all costs. For these helpers, allowing the edgy youth to build autonomy within their relationship limits the centrality of their own self and threatens their ability to construct the world with themselves at the center. Their need to personalize not only their interactions with others but even the experiences of others is compulsive; personalizing for these helpers serves the purpose of feeding that compulsion and has nothing at all to do with their relationship with young people. It is questionable whether these professional helpers are able to be in a relationship, at least in a manner that reflects characteristics such as partnership, transparency, mutual respect and concern for one another.

I raise this framework for understanding the purpose of personalizing because narcissism is a surprisingly common trait among professional helpers working with edgy youth, but it is not a topic or theme that is explored much within the communities of the helping professions. While there is an acknowledgment that professional helpers are subject to mental health challenges and behavioral traits that reflect the general society, there has not been much focus on the specific role of narcissism. Yet the helping professions generally, and specifically the youth serving professions, are inviting fields for those affected by narcissism. These are fields where the construction of stories and their development into life paths are welcomed and indeed required. Professional helpers are expected to be a role model for youth, presenting themselves to youth as persons who care while also maintaining authority in decision-making. Opportunities abound that demand the attention of young people while compulsively serving one's own need to be important, relevant and at the core of everything that happens.

How then do we recognize the narcissists among professional helpers in the youth-serving fields? One way is to listen closely to what helpers talk about when they relate their encounters with edgy youth to their colleagues. Are they talking about the relationship, the partnership, or even the young person at all? Or are they talking about themselves, what they might have said to the young person, how they might have responded in a particular situation? What appears to be the purpose of telling the story in the first place? Is it to reflect on the relationship with a young person, to see what might be done differently or what other possibilities for the future of the relationship might exist? Or is it to demonstrate to one and all how brilliant, how clear, and how competent one is? Who is the story really about?

Unlike the previous two characteristics of professional helpers, fearfulness and self-doubt, narcissism is dangerous and cannot be easily reframed, refined or reconstructed into something more positive, more youth-friendly or more substantive in terms of the engagement of edgy youth. Whereas both fearfulness and self-doubt really are indications of personal vulnerability, and the purpose of personalizing is simply to strengthen the helper's ability to be with edgy youth, narcissism is not at all about vulnerability. It is instead about the need to shine, to be noticed and to be validated chronically and without consideration of other perspectives or experiences. Narcissism seeks to render others invisible; in the case of edgy youth, it seeks to altogether negate their presence. From the perspective of edgy youth, narcissism is a microcosm of society at large; the young people's existence on the edge of the plateau is simply ignored, sidelined, marginalized and devalued. Likewise, when confronted with a narcissistic professional helper, young people quickly learn that their fate will be determined by the degree to which the narcissistic helper allows them to exist at all in the narrative about them, not by their actions or contributions to the discussions.

It becomes abundantly clear that personalizing, no matter how it is understood, has consequences for both the professional helper and for the edgy youth. These consequences range from potentially positive to entirely negative and destructive. In the next section of this chapter, I will explore some of the consequences of personalizing.

THE CONSEQUENCES OF PERSONALIZING

Having discussed both the reasons and purposes of personalizing, it is now necessary to explore its consequences in some detail. Why devote an entire chapter to the issues of personalizing if the consequences are of limited importance? I want to argue here that the consequences of personalizing are very significant, and are at the core of shaping what being with edgy youth could be if we remain reflective and acutely aware of the nature and extent of our own personalizing activities. At this point, it is also time to bring back the other meaning of personalizing, namely of taking things personally. After all, we will almost certainly be tempted to both personalize and take things personally many times each day in our everyday encounters with edgy youth.

I want to highlight eight specific consequences of personalizing and taking things personally. I am going to discuss each of these in the order of most positive to least positive. By positive, I mean that these consequences may hold opportunities for innovative approaches to being with edgy youth; by less positive, I mean consequences that will make being with edgy youth very difficult, and may sometimes result in a permanent rupture in our attempt to be with edgy youth. The eight consequences I will discuss below are:

- Transparency about vulnerability
- Giving power to edgy youth
- Limits and boundaries
- All talk, no listening
- Separation and disengagement
- Misleading diagnostics
- Negation of identity
- Us and them

Each of these consequences can be interpreted in many different ways, reflecting the frameworks for understanding the purpose of personalizing articulated in the previous section of the chapter. Nevertheless, I believe it is useful to think about each of these consequences, provide a brief description of what such a consequence might look like, and what it might mean from the perspective of edgy youth. It is always important to reflect on this latter aspect since in the end, the intentions of professional helpers and their helping systems are secondary to how these intentions are perceived and understood by the edgy youth themselves.

Transparency about Vulnerability

Although the terms personalizing and taking things personally are almost universally associated with performance issues on the part of professional helpers, and are seen as concerning on the part of supervisors and clinical managers, there is something profoundly positive about personalizing that is rarely articulated. In fact, it is hard to imagine an authentic relationship between two people, in any context, where personalizing does not happen at all. Such a purified relationship would appear as sterile, excessively formal and perhaps even artificial. In a dynamic, meaningful and evolving relationship, moments of taking things personally and of personalizing surely happen regularly from the perspective of both parties in the relationship. As we have already discussed earlier, edgy youth experience moments of fearfulness and self-doubt just as much as their professional helpers and while one hopes that these moments can be managed jointly and as elements of the relationship itself, realistically, one also has to expect bumps and setbacks in that process. Personalizing at some level is an indication of passion, interest, preoccupation and presence of the parties to the relationship. To the extent that personalizing reflects the vulnerabilities of the professional helper, openly displaying these to the young person is an indication of the helper's capacity for transparency. It is also an indication that the helper is prepared to take risks within the relationship, since such transparency provides opportunities for the young person to further exploit this vulnerability. It would be difficult indeed for a young person to make sense of a relationship in which the professional helper appears completely unaffected and immune to the actions and challenges of the young person. Such distance, predictability and sterility simply does not make for an interesting relationship in which both parties have room to explore and discover themselves and each other.

Being with edgy youth requires a degree of authenticity that cannot be achieved by pretending to be perfect; edgy youth are well versed in vulnerabilities and their impact on identity and behavior. Therefore, they often respond with interest and compassion when professional helpers personalize things as expressions of their vulnerability. As we will discuss later in the book, underestimating edgy youth, in terms of their capacity to respond meaningfully to the ups and down of human relationships, is one of the reasons why we often seem to dismiss the benefits of personalizing and focus on its challenges instead.

Giving Power to Edgy Youth

Perhaps somewhat counter-intuitively, personalizing can also have the effect of empowering, or giving power, to edgy youth. On the one hand, we have already discussed the disempowering aspects of personalizing and even the potentially identity-negating impacts. On the other hand, allowing edgy youth some insight into our vulnerabilities provides opportunities for them to lead the exploration of our limits and experiences. Within the relationship, professional helpers spend much time and effort trying to uncover the experiences of edgy youth and how they can make meaning of those experiences. Personalizing on the part of the professional helper provides opportunities for edgy youth to do the same with the helper. At least where helpers know better than to build walls around themselves, they can allow edgy youth to uncover their reasons and purposes of personalizing, thereby providing priceless avenues for mutuality within the relationship.

It is always important to consider the other side of the processes and issues encountered in being with edgy youth. We might think of this other side as being with professional helpers from the perspective of edgy youth. When we do so, it becomes readily apparent that edgy youth are always engaged in and indeed forced to personalize their experiences in being with professional helpers. It is only through personalizing that edgy youth can construct pathways for self-exploration and discovery. To do so, however, they must relinquish considerable control and trust that the professional helper will not misguide them into wrong directions or painful places. This process certainly can be disempowering as it firmly establishes a hierarchical component within the helper-youth relationship. From the young person's perspective, finding openings to guide the helper in his or her process of self-exploration and discovery restores some of the power differential that is inherently present in our being with them.

We have to be mindful of the tenuous relationship between personalizing and power. Without doubt, personalizing can also have a profoundly disempowering impact and marginalize the experiences of the young person so that the professional helper's experiences can take center stage. As we have already alluded to above, the helper maintains considerable power by having greater opportunities to speak about the young person to others than vice versa. Nevertheless, in spite of these risks and ambiguities embedded in the relationship between personalizing and power, opportunities for empowerment of young people ought not to be ignored either.

Limits and Boundaries

Another consequence of personalizing is the entrenchment of limits and boundaries within the relationship between helper and youth. This is a difficult consequence to evaluate because there clearly are both positive and negative aspects associated with limits and boundaries. Particularly in the context of boundaries, we can identify dialectical dynamics related to personalizing. On the one hand, the move to re-cast the experiences of a young person through the helper's own experiences and values will limit the opportunities for the young person to explore and discover his or her own experiences and their meaning. At the same time, imposing ownership over young people's stories will place firm boundaries on the degree of partnership with respect to responding to the purposes of personalizing. In effect, imposing such ownership on the part of the helper sends a message to the young person that whatever the issue might be, the young person no longer has access to exploring it or responding to it. The control has now shifted entirely to the professional helper, leaving the young person to observe from the periphery and to wait and see what will happen.

On the other hand, personalizing also opens the professional helper's world to the young person, and boundaries may well become blurry when the helper begins to relate or acknowledge personal experiences and values in ways that place demands on the relationship that are well outside of the expectations of the young person. This happens frequently when professional helpers personalize the lack of responsiveness of edgy youth and begin to express their frustrations as well as their insecurities and possibly even anger to the young person. Boundaries become blurred and even unhealthy because the young person suddenly finds himself or herself confronted with a professional helper exposing his or her personal issues, at the expense of focusing on the relationship with the young person. In these kinds of situations, personalizing can result in one of two outcomes: either the young person altogether removes himself or herself from the helper and terminates the relationship or the young person feels compelled to take on the role of helper while the professional helper is sorting through his or her issues and emotions. In either scenario, the consequences of personalizing on the part of the professional helper are significant and can potentially alter the ways that being with edgy youth might unfold. A reflective approach to responding to the boundary consequences of personalizing on the part of the helper would seek to ensure that boundaries are co-created as part of the evolving relationship. In this way, when episodes of personalizing appear unexpectedly, there is already a transparent framework for both helper and young person, both in terms of understanding how to manage these boundaries and what such boundaries mean in the context of the relationship.

All Talk, No Listening

The art of listening to and observing edgy youth in their everyday experiences is a core element of being with edgy youth. Indeed, without spending much time and effort listening and observing, professional helpers are not really being with edgy youth; instead, they are imposing their own needs and activities on the space of edgy youth as well as those that might be required by their employer, the program or the specific service they are there to provide. Personalizing seriously threatens the art of listening. When professional helpers seek to re-cast the experiences of young people in relation to their own experiences and through the filter of their own values, they stop listening and observing edgy youth and begin to construct their own realities. Personalizing is really about the act of talking, taking, and imposing, leaving virtually no room at all for listening, observing and allowing things to unfold.

The act of personalizing takes considerable energy and concentration. Unlike listening to edgy youth relate their experiences in a way that corresponds to their language preferences and their personal value systems, personalizing such experiences requires an active and real-time translation of the young person's story into language that makes sense to the helper and values that the helper can relate to and endorse. This process not only distracts the helper from actually listening to the nuances of the young person's story, but it also inherently changes that story in its substance and meaning. Young people are left feeling largely dismissed and ignored, while the professional helper has gained nothing in terms of understanding the young person.

Professional helpers can mitigate the impact of this particular consequence by reminding themselves of the first consequence of personalizing discussed above. By being transparent about one's vulnerabilities and inviting a joint exploration of that vulnerability, professional helpers can at least ensure that the talking inherently connected to the process of personalizing involves the young person as well and is not entirely unidirectional. Still, even such transparency cannot change the fact that the conversation will reflect the needs of the helper, rather than the experiences of the young person. In order to ensure that these experiences are at the center of being with edgy youth, professional helpers must invest time and energy into listening, rather than talking.

Separation and Disengagement

A common consequence of personalizing on the part of professional helpers is the increasing separation creeping into the helper-youth relationship as well as the incrementally more overt disengagement on the part of the young person. As I have emphasized on several occasions already, edgy youth are quite adept at identifying a helper's need to personalize, and they know well that helpers who personalize issues and themes they encounter while being with edgy youth are not likely going to be of much value to them. They won't have the capacity to listen to the full story the young people want to tell, and they won't have the patience to allow the youth to explore and discover whatever path might work for them. Instead, the experience of being with a personalizing professional helper is one in which edgy youth are pressured to succumb to control and compliance expectations that enforce values and story lines corresponding to the center, rather than the edge.

The consequence of disengagement is not only one initiated by the youth. Personalizing on the part of the helper is often a conscious approach to avoid engagement. So long as the issues and themes encountered in being with edgy youth are re-framed to fit the personal worldview and context of the helper, there is really no need to engage with the young person on any terms that are unfamiliar or pose any sort of risk. This consequence, therefore, is not only a consequence of personalizing but also the outcome of an avoidance strategy that helpers who are unable to see the value of life on the edge utilize regularly. The result is a helper-youth relationship that is devoid of any meaningful substance and that continues to exist rather than to evolve. This consequence cements the prioritization of coexistence over being with edgy youth.

The nature of disengagement is such that it perpetuates the process of personalizing on the part of the professional helper. The latter gets increasingly frustrated that the young person is not engaging in the program or service offered, and personalizes this disengagement on the part of the young person by disengaging him or herself. We can see then how as the consequences of personalizing become increasingly negative, they also begin to become self perpetuating, making it difficult to restore partnership in the helper-youth relationship.

Misleading Diagnostics

Even more significant and potentially destructive than separation and disengagement is the consequence of personalizing that one might term "misleading diagnostics". Professional helpers are often called upon to assess the emotional, mental, developmental and behavioral status of edgy youth. Their assessments are typically informal, simply based on observations of recent interactions between helper and young person and not on any sort of verifiable assessment measure or tool. In doing so, helpers are really assessing their own experience of the relationship with the young person. Not surprisingly, helpers who personalize their encounters with edgy youth will be assessing these through the filter of their own values and experiences which may or may not have any resemblance to what is happening for the young person. Consequently, the information given to other helpers or helping systems involved in the young person's life will be corrupted by the helper's personalizing habits or needs. The consequences of having wrong information, assessments or even diagnoses imposed on young people are potentially life changing. A particular service may be imposed or denied based on such reports.

It is in this context that the consequences of personalizing take on their most negative features. Being with edgy youth exposes helpers to a wide range of possible strengths and vulnerabilities of the youth; discovering these requires the ability to allow edgy youth to explore and present themselves as they deem appropriate. Personalizing the actions or lack of actions of the youth will limit the helper's ability to see and experience the full potential of the young people. Instead, the helper will experience his or her reaction, based on his or her personal values, to the young person''s activities. Reporting on one's own reactions is hardly the same as assessing the actions of another person in their proper context of that person's expressions of identity, values and competencies. Perhaps more importantly, we are now exposing the dangers of personalizing to their full extent. Most helpers are aware when they are personalizing and yet rarely have the courage to acknowledge this as a limitation of their assessments or diagnostic pronouncements. Only those helpers with the intent and desire to evolve their relationship with youth to a full-fledged partnership are likely to seek out feedback on the extent of their personalizing and ask for assistance from supervisors, mentors or colleagues to mitigate the impact of their personalizing whenever possible.

Negation of Identity

Edgy youth work hard to build their identities. Given the hardship, abuse, neglect, abandonment and other traumatic experiences in their lives, building an identity that works for them is no simple task. For most edgy youth, behavior and identity are easily separated. From the perspective of edgy youth, one's identity is not linked to one's everyday activities. Edgy youth have discovered that building an identity that is forward-looking and based on their hopes and dreams, rather than their current social and emotional context, is a more realistic approach to moving forward under the circumstances. As a result, many edgy youth appear to be stuck in a particular place of behavior and achievement when, in fact, they have done considerable work preparing themselves mentally and emotionally for the next steps in their life journey.

The consequence of personalizing on the part of professional helpers can often be a negation of the edgy youth's identity. As helpers personalize the behaviors, actions or inactions of the youth, they begin to form assessments and diagnoses that are based entirely on their interpretation of what they see. In fact, these helpers are not accessing the latest (but invisible) developments with respect to the young person's identity at all. Instead, they evaluate only what they see and begin to impose characteristics of an identity that corresponds to their expectations and also to the expectations of the center, mirrored by the agencies and organizations in the youth-serving fields.

For most edgy youth, identity is their most valuable possession, one that is entirely theirs. Dismissing the full complexity of the identity of edgy youth negates their being. Far from being with edgy youth, personalizing carries with it the consequence of negating the very person we are trying to be with.

Us and Them

The eighth and final consequence of personalizing on the part of professional helpers I want to briefly explore is the development of a culture of "us and them". This consequence is really the accumulated effect of all of the previous ones, especially those that result in a negation, dismissal or denial of the unique identities of edgy youth. From the perspective of edgy youth, personalizing on the part of professional helpers reinforces the separation of those who reflect the center and those who are from the edge. In spite of all of the expressed goodwill, the good intentions and the seemingly positive offers made by helping systems, when particular professional helpers begin to personalize their experiences in being with edgy youth, the latter lose whatever confidence and trust that might have been gained, such that being together really means more than finding the path to conformity. As far as edgy youth are concerned (and I believe they are right on this one), being together is neither about the helper nor about the youth, but instead, it is quite clearly about the relationship between helper and youth. It is only when both parties in this relationship allow themselves to be guided by that alternate relationship, vulnerabilities such as fearfulness and self-doubt, notwithstanding that we can really begin to talk about the concept of being with edgy youth.

NO SINGLE PERSON IS THAT IMPORTANT!

I devoted an entire chapter to explore the issues and themes of personalizing on the part of professional helpers because I believe that this issue alone has been the greatest obstacle to finding ways of really being with edgy youth. In my experience, there are two kinds of professional helpers who are simply not good enough: the one who personalizes everything and feels that this is just fine, and the one who knows that personalizing things can have negative consequences and therefore, believes him or herself to never personalize anything. Both of these types of helpers are off the mark. As we discussed in this chapter, the first type often turns out to be a helper affected by narcissism; these kinds of professional helpers are not very helpful, and if they cannot determine that for themselves, it is imperative that supervisors, mentors or colleagues with a healthier sense of self actually point it out to them. The other type is simply not realistic, perhaps because of an over-estimation of their own capacities, or an under-estimation of the astuteness of edgy youth. These youth know that personalizing can never be entirely avoided. In reality, personalizing our experiences with edgy youth is perfectly natural and unavoidable; edgy youth will also personalize their experiences with us. It is what we do with this simple reality that matters. We may have common reasons for personalizing things, but we must begin to distinguish between good purposes and not so good purposes, and we must also remain conscious of the range of consequences that personalizing things may carry.

Ultimately, it is important to remember that no one among us is so important that edgy youth can be robbed of their identity, dismissed as wrong, labeled as incompetent or marginalized in their own story. The need to feel important in being with edgy youth is natural; the compulsion to measure this importance by personalizing our experiences in such a way that we always find ourselves at the center of the story is a big problem, and in this chapter I have sought to describe and label this problem as clearly as possible. I have also sought to point out that, even in the context of personalizing, things are not always as simple as they may at first appear. As I argued earlier in this chapter, there is nothing wrong with being personally invested in the process of being with edgy youth. Indeed, the complete absence of personalizing raises some suspicions about the helper's commitment to the youth. Is it really possible to be completely unaffected on a personal level when so much of the work takes place in the context of relationships and being together?

Having explored the issues and themes of personalizing in such detail, we can now move on to the more positive task of really thinking about how we might not only be with edgy youth in a way that is constructive and meaningful for everyone affected, but also democratic, partnership-based, transparent and authentic in every way.

Chapter 4

BECOMING PRESENT

It would seem that there can be no more obvious and simple concept associated with being with edgy youth than being present. After all, how could one be with edgy youth by being absent? Virtually all programs and services developed for edgy youth require professional helpers to physically show up and to interact with the youth face to face. In this way, there is no doubt that being present is a core component of what professional helpers do every day. However, if we reflect a little more carefully about the concept of presence, its many different manifestations, and its impact, given the new technologies that allow for a virtual presence, we may discover that the concept of presence, and specifically of being present, is a very complex concept. It turns out that it is possible to be present even when absent, and it is also possible to be absent even while one is standing right there in front of the young person. It also turns out that virtually everything else that happens in a helping relationship relies, to a large degree, on the success of being present in the life of the other, *as determined by the other*. Thus, professional helpers encounter yet another challenge here: while they may take the steps necessary to be present in the life of an edgy youth, whether or not they actually are present is not for them to say. Edgy youth get the final word on this, which is why being present is ultimately not the outcome of the helper's actions, but rather an indicator of the relationship's status.

Edgy youth often doubt that we care enough to maintain our presence in their lives; at best, we will be in and out of their lives based on what works for our schedules, what is convenient in the moment, and what we might be required to do by our bosses or by the programs and services we are mandated to provide. It is not that we, as professional helpers, care neither about being present nor make an appropriate effort to be present. Instead, the issue is simply that the concept of being present is too often taken for granted and equated with the idea of physically showing up to be with the youth. Employers, service systems, programs and services rarely ask how one might be present in the lives of the youth. Instead, they focus on activities, measurable outcomes and the performance of both the helpers and the young people. In other words, our being with edgy youth almost always takes place in a very formal context that is impacted by the logistics of employment law, organizational needs and professional issues.

In this chapter, I want to get straight to the heart of the matter of being with edgy youth. Specifically, I want to critically evaluate the ways in which we have become accustomed to making our presence felt by young people and why these ways are not adequate and sometimes counterproductive when dealing with edgy youth. I will begin by examining the formal context of our being with edgy youth and its shortcomings, and propose that rather than assuming our presence to be relevant by default, we must accept a path to becoming present by transcending much of the formalities that govern our work.

FORMAL PRESENCE

One of the reasons that there has been so little attention paid to being with edgy youth in the human services literature and the practice settings where edgy youth receive services is that the concept of "being" is generally viewed as a passive concept. More than just passive, however, it is also viewed as a concept that is difficult to formalize, to professionalize and to measure. In our world of technocratic rules and bureaucratic procedure, concepts such as "being" are real challenges, and they are generally dismissed in favor of more quantifiable concepts that are related to "doing", including concepts such as engagement, intervention and treatment. All of these kinds of concepts come with extensive research and analysis in the human services literature, and we have some sense of what kinds of "doing" activities might lead to positive outcomes (we call this the evidence base). Much more important than outcomes, however, is that we are able to wrap organizational systems and employment rules around such concepts; in other words, we can imagine the logistical framework within which such concepts can be operationalized. A closer look at how we deliver services to edgy youth, regardless of setting or context, reveals, over all else, the centrality of logistical considerations.

Logistical Considerations

The logistics of working (rather than being) with edgy youth include a range of foci, including the all-important employment rules and regulations. Professional helpers are employees of an agency, or an organization and their deployment with edgy youth is governed by employment law and by organizational human resource policies that significantly impact the nature of their work with the youth. Indeed, we rarely pay enough attention to the extent to which such rules limit what we are able to do with edgy youth, even when it is readily apparent that a different approach is needed. The first example of such limitations, resulting from logistical considerations, is the scheduling of the professional helper. It is almost always the case that the job of working with edgy youth comes with a set schedule that limits the number of hours worked per week as well as when those hours are worked. Indeed, it is important to recognize that professional helpers work based on their schedule, rather than based on the needs or wants of the edgy youth. From the very beginning, then, being with edgy youth is centered around the logistical world of the professional helper, rather than the everyday experiences of the edgy youth.[1]

As part of scheduling, other logistical considerations appear that again support the social, economic and personal world of the professional helper, often without any consideration to the experiences of the edgy youth. Professional helpers earn vacation time and they may be replaced during their vacations by whoever might be available to work with the young person. This kind of approach exposes the rhetorical nature of our emphasis on relationships. How can we consider a replacement helper as an adequate substitute to the helper who is connected to the young person? This sort of juggling of helper-youth relationships is, in part, a function of the case load approach that is often developed to organize the work of youth-serving agencies. Professional helpers are assigned a certain number of young people to work with; when the helper is not available due to vacation time, sickness or for any other reasons, that caseload is either distributed to other helpers or a new helper is hired and takes over the caseload all together. As an organizational tool, case loads are extraordinarily effective ways of ensuring

---

[1] It should be noted that there are services and approaches to helping others that attempt to mitigate the inevitable impact of logistical considerations. In the context of being with edgy youth, for example, street outreach services or even in-home family support services often try very hard to adjust the service to the young person's or even the family's life style. See for example Garfat (2003).

an equitable distribution of work load and uninterrupted service provision as workers change. From the perspective of being with edgy youth, however, case loads render the process of "being" fragmented, packaged and overly formalized.

The logistics of working with edgy youth are not limited to human resource considerations and work schedules. Just as important as these is the emphasis on recording and documenting the work that unfolds every day. In many service settings, it is not the being with edgy youth that is considered as the work, but instead it is the completeness of the documentation of having met the requirements related to whatever agency mandate might be in place. In other words, professional helpers are presumed to have been with edgy youth if their documentation in the case files is complete and meets externally set standards. It is not surprising that for many professional helpers, the pressure to meet those standards results in an approach to being with edgy youth that specifically facilitates the meeting of the standards, rather than one that is explorative and not pre-determined by any requirements or expectations that are externally imposed. Therefore, the authenticity of being with the youth is limited and often non-existent. While logistics alone create very significant obstacles to being with edgy youth in authentic and meaningful ways, professional issues further add to these challenges and are just as difficult for the professional helper to overcome.

Professional Issues

We all bring something to being with someone else, but unfortunately what professional helpers bring to being with edgy youth is often an overwhelming and difficult to understand professional context that includes boundaries, role descriptions, multi-disciplinary teams, values and ethics. One of the disadvantages of the professionalization of many of the disciplines concerned with youth is that there are now more rules and expectations related to the professional context of being with edgy youth than ever before. Whether professional helpers encounter youth in residential care settings, in the community or in family homes, the reality is that before the helpers ever determine how to proceed, much of their work's foundation has already been set by managers, supervisors, policies and procedures, and professional rules and cultures that claim to separate right from wrong, correct from incorrect and useful from useless.

Boundaries, more than any other professional issue, often predetermine what is possible in our being with edgy youth. Increasingly, the expectation of firmly set boundaries to be maintained by the professional helper has become embedded in the human services fields. By boundaries, what is usually meant is a clear separation of the professional helper as a person in his or her own right and as the ambassador of a program or service. Any indication that the helper allows a young person access to his or her personal world is often seen as highly problematic, possibly dangerous and can even result in the termination of the professional helper altogether. The personal world is said to include just about anything that humanizes the helper, including any personal relationships outside of the agency, stories reflecting personal experiences, demonstrations of personal habits and preferences, sharing of personal items, and a host of other things and activities that, under any other circumstances, are considered perfectly normal, if not central requirements, of relationships.

From the perspective of edgy youth, these kinds of boundaries are highly problematic. Given the mistrust and suspicion edgy youth typically foster in relation to helping professionals and their helping systems, being confronted with impenetrable walls between themselves and their helpers does little to mitigate this mistrust and suspicion. Edgy youth are not likely to feel authentically and meaningfully engaged in a one way relationship in which they are expected to have no boundaries at all, while their helpers can pretend to be able to shed their humanity and act strictly as ambassadors for the program. From the perspective of the professional helper, on the other hand, employer expectations about the maintenance of boundaries serve to intensify the fearfulness and self-doubt explored in the previous chapter. The reality faced by professional helpers is that their approach to setting boundaries will come under scrutiny if the performance expectations of the young people do not correspond with what was laid out in their treatment plan, intervention plan or plan of care. From the start, therefore, the professional issues associated with the setting of boundaries create inherent fragility in the process of being with edgy youth because it enhances the vulnerabilities of the professional helper that are always present anyway.

Yet another professional issue that features very centrally in the process of being with edgy youth is that it is not always clear *who* is being with the edgy youth. While the assignment of a professional helper to an edgy youth seems to suggest that there are two parties to the relationship, things are often a little more complicated. This is because the professional helper almost never has the ability to be with the edgy youth in isolation; more commonly, the helper is a member of a multi-disciplinary team[2], therefore having responsibilities to report back to that team about their observations and experiences with the edgy youth. The team, in turn, will provide feedback and input associated with how the helper is to engage the young person, so that substantial elements of the helper's being with the edgy youth are really not at all functions of the helper-youth relationship, but instead of the youth-helping system relationship, whereby that systems includes a range of professionals some of whom the young person may or may not even know. Further complicating matters is the pressure to maintain a unified front and strong consistency in the implementation of treatment or intervention plans, such that the professional helper is forced to engage the young person in ways that may or may not correspond to his or her preferences. Even worse, partly because of the professional boundaries discussed above and partly because of the hierarchical structures of multi-disciplinary teams, the helper cannot even openly discuss apparent deviations from his values and ethics to serve the commands of the team. From the perspective of the edgy youth, then, the relationship with the professional helper can never be fully trusted, even if the helper has acted with integrity and in ways that have captured the interest and trust of the young person. Given the background presence of the multi-disciplinary team, the professional helper assigned to the edgy youth is never the complete representation of the services or programs imposed on the young person.

Team approaches to being with edgy youth are further complicated by job descriptions and role assignments that are often ambiguous. Professional helpers assigned to being with edgy youth have imposed limitations upon them, in terms of the kinds of issues and themes they are allowed to address and even the kinds of activities they can initiate. Decision-making is often very hierarchically organized, and it is the professional with the least direct contact with the young person who generally has the highest level of decision-making authority. From an organizational perspective, this structure is important in order to maintain high levels of accountability and also to ensure that risk management strategies are in place and any liability exposure is mitigated. Unfortunately, these kinds of formal structures and ways of organizing the context of being with edgy youth are alien to the everyday

---

[2] Multi-disciplinary treatment or intervention teams, in the context of working with edgy youth, typically seek to include representation from the service sectors where edgy youth often are involved, such as child protection, children's mental health, education, youth justice, and health. Such teams also try and deliver services reflecting professional perspectives, ranging from social work to psychiatry. Although the idea of multi-disciplinary teams is generally regarded as a good one, such teams are not without problems. See for example Salhani & Charles (2007).

experience of these youth and, in many respects, serve to widen the gulf between the center and the edge. When confronted with structures and processes that are this far removed from their everyday reality and experiences, most edgy youth simply retreat and turn back toward the edge as a place of comfort and familiarity.

Even outside of the influences from higher placed team members or policies and procedures, professional helpers are influenced by professional issues related to values and ethics, some reflecting their personal inclinations, others reflecting standards set by professional associations and codes of ethics developed for particular disciplines. Values and ethics are often highly prescriptive in terms of boundaries and confidentiality issues as well as in terms of issues of judgment, tolerance and acceptance. The imposition of values and ethics that are developed and strongly embedded outside of the relationship with edgy youth again serves to limit what is possible within that relationship. It is notable that edgy youth are not often asked about their values and ethics in being with professional helpers, and are instead expected to conform to those expressed or quietly imposed by the helpers. The lack of democratic content and the obvious disempowerment usually go unacknowledged. While this is an obvious issue in the relationships between helper and youth, it is less obvious but just as relevant in the way in which such values and ethics are embedded in specific programs and services, affecting helper-youth relationships on an on-going basis.

Program and Services Considerations

The formality of service systems within the youth-serving sectors is reflected in the logistical and professional considerations discussed above, and it is further promoted by the program and service considerations that are tied to outcomes and evaluation. With increasing intensity, *being* with edgy youth has been rendered largely irrelevant, and what matters instead is the data that is being collected and analyzed about the youth. Outcome data reflects the performance of young people pre- and post- service provision; it says nothing at all about the process of being with edgy youth. In fact, I would argue that the drive to generate more and more outcome data actually serves to discourage professional helpers from being with edgy youth. This is the case as the investment of time and effort, in relation to being with edgy youth, cannot be captured by outcome data and can, therefore, easily appear as dead weight. In modern service provision, the professional helper is often little more than the tool used to implement helping strategies that have been proven effective elsewhere (effective in relation to particular outcomes deemed desirable). While the rhetoric of such service provision continues to emphasize the importance of helper-youth relationships, the practice does not, and indeed, the sought after product, outcome data, also does not focus on that relationship at all.

One of the great challenges of evidence-based approaches to service provision is that these are based on aggregate performance outcomes of groups of young people. Like any aggregated data, there is little to be learned for those young people for whom a particular intervention did not work. For example, if the outcome data of an intervention tells us that 80% of young people subject to an intervention experience significant progress in a particular performance area, we learn nothing at all about how to assist the 20% who did not experience this progress. Chances are that it is those 20% who make up the group of edgy youth we are concerned with here. The focus on data collection and outcome measurement, although beneficial for the alignment of services based on what we know might work, serves to reduce the opportunities for professional helpers to be with edgy youth. Instead, edgy youth will produce the outcome data reflecting failure as a counterweight to the data reflecting success. So long as the success data outweighs the failure data, we can assume edgy youth to continue to experience marginalization under this approach of program and service delivery.

Although it is patently obvious that the evidence we have been collecting over the years for what works does not include all young people in need of assistance, we have not been able to adjust our programs and services to ensure the inclusion of those young people for whom the evidence does not speak. This again points to the limitations imposed by the formality of the service systems for young people. Increasingly, the funding of these systems depends on the outcomes they are able to demonstrate and the nature of the outcomes that are deemed acceptable are those that correspond to the values and preferences of the center. These are outcomes related to performance and growth, as reflected in pre-determined time frames that typically correspond to the fiscal cycles of either public or private funding sources. Within this kind of a framework, it is indeed difficult to develop approaches to being with edgy youth that both meet the requirements of funders and stimulate the interest of edgy youth to consider engaging with professional helpers.

FORMALITY AND ABSENCE

It is difficult to be present within the context of a formal approach to helping others. This is not a criticism of formality, but it does hint at some of the challenges that formality presents to the concept of becoming present, especially when one is trying to become present in the life of an edgy youth. Almost all programs and services for edgy youth start with the best of intentions, and most recognize in their design the importance of accepting the uniqueness of each young person to be served. The rhetoric of personalization, or customization and individualized service designs, however, quickly loses its connection to actual service provision once logistical, professional, program structures and routines become integrated into the everyday life of the program or service. In reality, most edgy youth quickly realize that their uniqueness is of little interest to professional helpers, who tend to be preoccupied with serving the needs and priorities of their employers. A culture of how to be with edgy youth develops based on a broad set of assumptions about how edgy youth might best be changed to become productive and conforming citizens. Within this culture, the edgy youth who fail to follow the expected trajectory of change are blamed for their failure or have their readiness for the program or service questioned. Ultimately, a truth develops that postulates failure as reflections of the young people, rather than limitations of the programs and services provided.

In spite of the provision of human resources and the assignment of professional helpers to edgy youth, formality often results in the entrenchment of absence, rather than presence. Absence, in this context, means that in spite of a physical presence of and on-going interaction between a professional helper and a young person, the experience of the young person is not enriched by the helper's presence. Instead, the helper's presence serves to institutionalize and routinize the resistance of edgy youth in their interactions and engagement with programs and services. Edgy youth either ignore or refuse to absorb the helping actions of the professional helper and instead tolerate the helper's presence when doing so is to their advantage and ignoring it when it is deemed unpleasant. We can certainly see this dynamic unfolding in structured settings such as group homes and special school programs where youth often have moments of seemingly positive interaction and engagement with the professional staff, and then suddenly disappear for days at a time. For many professional helpers, it is difficult not to take this kind of rejection personally; in fact, edgy youth are not really rejecting the particular professional helper, but only the formal context in which the helper must deliver his or her services. Many professional helpers simply do not realize that in following the commands of program structures and employment routines and requirements, they are contributing to their absence in the helper-young person relationship more so than their presence. This makes being with edgy youth very difficult indeed.

BECOMING PRESENT

It is becoming increasingly clear in thinking about the limitations posed by formalities in our being with edgy youth that what is really required is something other than formality. It is not obvious, however, what this something other might be. We can dismiss the idea that we should simply do away with formal requirements altogether because this is simply not realistic at a time when helping professionals are seeking to gain greater recognition for their work and expertise, while also trying very hard to improve their working conditions. The last thing professional helpers from all disciplines want is to be seen as individuals who can be asked to work any time of the day, for unlimited hours, and under any sort of circumstances without any recourse to employment law, organizational policies and procedures or professional rules of conduct. However, the increasing attention to such issues on the part of professional helpers, combined with a rapidly accelerating commitment to evidence-based practices and outcome-oriented interventions on the part of employer and service providers more generally, threaten the integrity of being with edgy youth. The youth recognize that they are mere pawns in a much larger and more complex constellation of variables that even their professional helpers cannot fully grasp, much less control.

If we cannot altogether dismiss formality and adopt a completely informal system of professional help for edgy youth in its place, we must find an alternative approach to being with edgy youth that allows for formality to co-exist, both with informal and alternative approaches of coming together with others. We can do this by transcending formality instead of abandoning it. The concept of "transcending" implies that we maintain the fundamental premises of formality, including considerations of logistics, professional issues, and program and service objectives and goals, but we also consider opportunities for constituting these fundamental premises of formality differently. One of our goals will be to do so more democratically, so that edgy youth find their stake in this process and have opportunities to control the direction of our coming together and of our becoming present.

Sharing of Logistical Burdens

Although edgy youth are significantly impacted by the logistical considerations of helping systems, they are not often included in discussions of how to manage these. Indeed, there is a long standing assumption in the helping professions that the logistical issues impacting the helpers are to be kept at an arm's length from the young people; these issues are adult issues and therefore ought to be resolved among the adults involved. As much as this is a well-intended position to take, it is also a position that perpetuates the marginalization of edgy youth in the helping process as well as their suspicions that they will never be recognized as equal partners within the helper-youth dyad. In fact, there is really no reason at all why the logistical considerations of service provision, including issues such as scheduling, coverage for vacation time, team meetings and case load determinations should be kept secret, or at least far away, from the young people who will be impacted by the relevant decisions. Edgy youth typically are much more engaged when they have the relevant information than when they do not have any information at all. Furthermore, they are quite capable of contributing to problem-solving when necessary. What edgy youth often do not appreciate very much are exaggerated protective measures that serve to exclude them in those matters that significantly affect them.

A first step in becoming present, then, is to be transparent about logistical issues wherever these appear and whenever these threaten to impact, even moderately, on the young people with whom professional helpers are engaged. Beyond simply informing the youth about such logistical considerations, it is entirely appropriate, and indeed meaningful, to also share some of the emotional consequences of the logistical considerations. Professional helpers can and should express their frustrations with logistical requirements so long as such frustrations are expressed as evidence of a desire for something different, rather than a request for support and guidance from the youth. From the perspective of edgy youth, professional helpers who pretend to be entirely satisfied with the logistics of their role may well lack integrity and reliability in terms of sharing information and possible consequences of ever-changing logistics as the helper-youth relationship develops.

Democratizing Togetherness

A key element of coming together and becoming present in the lives of edgy youth is to allow for deviations from the treatment plan or intervention plan as it was developed by the multi-disciplinary team. Edgy youth need to find opportunities to shape their involvements with others, including professional helpers, in order to test out the reliability of those helpers as well as their entitlements in terms of decision-making and choosing their own path. One of the things edgy youth learn quickly as they grow accustomed to their life on the edge is that the loss of opportunity for self determination constitutes a major threat to their well-being and safety. Having been disappointed by helpers, care givers and others interveners on many occasions, the need to maintain control over what happens next is significant and must be taken seriously.

A democratizing approach to being with edgy youth and to becoming present allows for the youth to determine the agenda, including everyday activities, as well as longer term goals and objectives, alongside the professional helper, rather than as a form of resistance to the helper. As much as the professional helper serves as an ambassador of the program or service that employs him or her, he or she must also serve as a representative of the young person. Therefore, they mitigate some of the time and performance pressures imposed by these programs and services. Professional helpers who fail to accept this part of the helping role will struggle to become present with edgy youth as the latter will quickly move to entrench their absence by simply leaving the service altogether or adopting the "take what is useful and ignore the rest" approach to being engaged.

From the perspective of edgy youth, a democratic approach to being together and to becoming present is one that feels like they matter within the relationship not only as subjects of intervention and change, but as real human beings with much to contribute to their own future and to the shared experience of the relationship with the professional helpers. Democratic approaches are characterized by patience and openness to different experiences and different routes toward growth and change. Edgy youth will often test the interest of professional helpers in their everyday experiences and the helper's acceptance of experiences that may not correspond entirely to their value systems and sensibilities. Specifically, edgy youth will want to know that allowing the professional helper to become present in their lives will not negate their decision-making authority in relation to their own affairs; instead, they hope to not only gain guidance and advice from the helper that confirms their decision-making authority but also allows for a sharing of such authority with the helper in situations where the helper may be able to advance the interests of the young person more effectively than the young person.

Assigning a Core Role to Youth

Very much along the same lines as democratizing togetherness, it is critical that youth be assigned important roles in the on-going relationship with the professional helper and also in the everyday interaction with the programs and services that are being offered to them. Edgy youth typically don't shy away from accepting gifts, free opportunities for activities, and support and guidance that they recognize to be useful. They are also quick to take such things for what they are: momentary opportunities to be exploited as much as possible, but not necessarily to be integrated into their own framework for memories and learning experiences.

In order for edgy youth to take responsibility for their experiences and to feel like they have a stake in fully considering every aspect of such experiences, they need to feel like they have an important role in that experience. It is only when young people are given opportunities to affect what happens next that they begin to explore the possibilities for experiences that otherwise might have been taken for granted. To the extent that professional helpers take on the role of delivering pre-packaged programs and services to edgy youth, based on an agency's commitment to evidence-based practices, there is still a need to incorporate a central role for the youth into the delivery of such programs, even if this derails the required trajectory for the intervention. The need for young people to co-own the intervention supersedes the commands of the evidence.

Negotiating Boundaries

This, then, brings us to another area where formality needs to be transcended, rather than dismissed. Clearly, the issue of boundaries represents one of the most complex elements of being with edgy youth. On the one hand, setting and managing boundaries are the skills that separate professional helpers from well-meaning friends and relatives. On the other hand, boundaries that are created based on a pre-determined policy or organizational culture principles completely fail to address the uniqueness of edgy youth as a group and of each young person as an individual. Therefore, transcending such pre-determined principles, in the process of boundary setting, requires a commitment to negotiating boundaries with the youth on an on-going basis. Indeed, in the context of boundary setting, professional helping systems have only very rarely considered the needs of the youth to set their own boundaries. Instead, there has always been an assumption that edgy youth ought not to have boundaries that might challenge the helper's authority and expertise in determining the most appropriate path for change and growth. As it turns out, however, edgy youth often have a very developed sense of boundaries, in relation to professional helpers, based on considerable experiences with helpers and their helping systems. It is critical, therefore, that boundaries between a professional helper and the edgy youth be negotiated over time, rather than imposed from the start. Boundaries are a defining element of becoming present and of being with edgy youth. Once we are able to acknowledge becoming present and being with edgy youth as a process, we will also be able to recognize that boundaries cannot be presented to edgy youth as a condition of coming together, but instead must be promoted as an area of negotiation between equal partners.

Transcending formality is one major step toward becoming present with edgy youth; it is not, however, the only necessary step. In addition to the elements of transcending formality discussed above, we also need to consider some other core assumptions about becoming present and being with edgy youth. One such core assumption relates to the predominance of physical presence as an indicator of presence. In the next section of this chapter, I want to propose that our physical presence with edgy youth is, secondary to our metaphorical or virtual presence in their lives. In order to make this argument, we have to contemplate the importance of transcending space in the professional helper-edgy youth relationship.

TRANSCENDING PHYSICAL SPACE

In most cases, professional helpers spend relatively little face to face time with the young people on their case loads. Logistical considerations typically require that such helpers divide their time among several clients, and also that some of the time allocated for their weekly work load is spent writing reports, attending team meetings and receiving supervision. In the end, it is quite typical for a professional helper to perhaps spend between two and ten hours per week with an edgy youth on his or her case load. Clearly, this creates challenges in terms of becoming present in a meaningful way in the life of the edgy youth. From the perspective of edgy youth, life on the edge is a seven day a week reality, and occasional encounters with a professional helper are not likely to change this or to have a significant impact if such impact is to be measured entirely on the basis of the face to face encounters.

Edgy youth, much like all young people, do not spend their living in only physical spaces, and it is essential that professional helpers find ways of accessing some of the other kinds of spaces where edgy youth might find themselves. In this section of the chapter, I want to highlight the importance of thinking about becoming present and being with edgy youth in such a way that it transcends the notion of space as a physical concept. In addition to physical spaces, edgy youth also find themselves living their lives in mental, relational and virtual spaces that can also be accessed by professional helpers (Gharabaghi & Stuart, 2012).

Mental Spaces

Whether it is about resentment about their situation or simply a function of having a lack of structure in their lives, edgy youth spend much time imagining themselves in a different context, living a different life and knowing different people. Like all young people (and adults too), edgy youth day dream, imagine all kinds of other worlds and develop a narrative for themselves based on substantially revised material contexts from their physical world. These narratives are very important if one wants to become present in the life of an edgy youth. To the extent that the youth create these narratives about themselves, they also find alternate roles for others involved in their lives, potentially including the professional helpers. These imagined stories are often more central in the young person's life than the life that we are able to observe; when professional helpers fail to find a role or a place within these imagined stories, they are absent from what can be a core element of the young person's everyday life experiences.

When professional helpers become present within the young person's imagined stories about themselves, they transcend the limitations of physical face to face encounters, and they become present in the life of the edgy youth, even when they are physically absent. The challenge of maintaining such a presence within the mental space of the young person is that the professional helper must absolve control over his or her role within the young person's story and allow the young person to direct the development of the helper's character within the story. In this way, becoming present in the mental space of an edgy youth also involves letting go of our frequent need for control. In so doing, we are inherently transcending some of the more formal ways of being present and allowing for alternative forms of presence and being with edgy youth to emerge and evolve.

Virtual Spaces

Yet another way of transcending our dependence on face to face interaction with edgy youth presents itself through the medium of technology. Over the past decade, e-mail, texting and social networking have become staples of communication at all levels of societal functioning. In spite of this, there continues to be considerable hesitation on the part of professional helpers to engage edgy youth through such technologies, and indeed many helping organizations continue to maintain rather restrictive policies about technology driven forms of engagement. Concerns about boundaries and a lack of control over what happens with information conveyed through cyberspace technologies have limited the use of virtual opportunities for becoming present in the lives of edgy youth.

It is notable that the use of such technologies for young people has generally proliferated rapidly and is typically not greeted with a great deal of concern by society at large. At the appropriate age, typically around 13 or 14 years, parents around the world, but certainly in North America, are happy to supply the technological gadgets necessary to stay in touch with their kids wherever they may be. Texting and social networking is common practice in parent-youth relationships, but it is viewed as dangerous territory in professional helper-edgy youth relationships.

Becoming present in the lives of edgy youth cannot exclude the virtual world. The reality is that the virtual world provides a particularly good fit for the life experiences of edgy youth. Not unlike living on the edge, living in a virtual world allows for a separation of the everyday experiences of marginalization and alienation on the part of young people in their traditional and orthodox spaces such as school, home, neighborhood and community center on the one hand, and the ability to recreate an identity and life that fits the hopes and aspiration of the young person on the other hand. From the perspective of the professional helper, therefore, accessing this virtual world, whether it be through associations on social networking sites, communication through texting or e-mail, or participation in gaming and simulation, is an essential step to finding presence in this aspect of the young person's life. Not unlike in the physical world, boundaries can still be negotiated jointly, allowing a voice and decision-making authority, for both the helper and the young person.

Relational Spaces

A final space that needs to be considered by professional helpers in their attempts to become present in the lives of edgy youth is the relational space occupied by the youth. Edgy youth experience a great deal of instability in their lives and often lack stable housing, access to schools, community programs, or other institutions and routines. As a result, whatever relationships that can be fostered by edgy youth often take on extraordinarily important roles in the lives of the young people. Often, peer-based relationships, relationships with family members, other professionals and a range of interested adults, provide familiar and comfortable relational spaces for edgy youth. Indeed, these are spaces to which edgy youth retreat once they detect a lack of safety or comfort in the physical spaces that are available through the programs and services offered to them.

The professional helping process itself, of course, requires a focus on relationships. Professional helpers are typically aware of the need to develop and continuously nurture an evolving relationship with the edgy youth assigned to them. Finding presence within the relational spaces of edgy youth is about more than merely forming relationships; it is more fundamentally about finding a presence in already existing relationships between the young person and his or her social connections, including peers, family, other professionals and interested adults. To be present in the life of an edgy youth requires some degree of familiarity with that young person's relationships and a connection to these relationships that is enduring and intimate. This means that the young person must be aware of the helper's connection to his or her relational spaces, and the helper becomes integrated into the everyday conversations within those relational spaces. The presence of the helper in the life of an edgy youth finds confirmation in the helper's presence in other relationships held and valued by that edgy youth.

GETTING CONNECTED

Up to this point, I have sought to emphasize the complexity of the everyday life experiences and life spaces of edgy youth and the resultant necessity on the part of professional helpers to find access to all of the spaces where young people live their lives. This includes the mental, virtual and relational spaces that, for many edgy youth, are really far more important than the physical spaces where they might find themselves on a day to day basis.

Becoming present in the life of an edgy youth is really about getting connected wherever possible. From the perspective of the professional helper, the goal is one of becoming entangled in the everyday experiences of the edgy youth without, however, taking over or disempowering the edgy youth by taking on an excessively dominant or central role. Becoming present requires a deep respect for the young person's right to develop his or her own narrative about himself or herself. Whatever story the young person wishes to tell, the professional helper wants to be present in that story and allow the young person to continue to evolve the story as they see fit. Doing so will require a very multi-faceted strategy of getting connected, involving paying attention to the social connections of the edgy youth and a willingness to become exposed to those connections; it will also involve finding multiple ways of communicating with the young person that transcend face to face communication and include communication within the virtual realm as well as the mental realm. Aside from the obvious technological tools that can be used to further these goals, other more old fashioned but equally effective tools include letter writing, sharing of notes, and providing transitional objects to the young person.

I want to be as explicit about the strategies of becoming present in the lives of edgy youth as possible; it is within these strategies that we can ascertain some of the complexities of being with edgy youth that professional helpers need to remain mindful of. To this end, I will briefly explore ten ways of measuring one's presence in the life of an edgy youth.

TEN WAYS OF MEASURING PRESENCE
WITH EDGY YOUTH

1. *What do you know about the youth?* It is helpful to ask oneself this question from time to time, even when we feel that we have a good

grasp on the social and personal history of the young person we are working with. In reality, formal systems impose their logistical needs and procedures not only on how we do things, but also on the kinds of things we learn about the young people on our case loads. It is common practice, for example, to either be given or to ascertain information about a young person's family background, their mental health diagnoses, their experiences of trauma and their performance in various settings, especially school. But are these really the kinds of things that help us understand and relate to a young person? From the perspective of young people generally and certainly from the perspective of edgy youth, there are a host of other things that matter as much and more in their everyday experiences of life, but that are not typically part of the official questionnaires, the intake interviews or the documentation on file for that young person. These kinds of things might include the young person's favorite kind of music or favorite song, special numbers for which the young person has an association, phobias or chronic fears for which there are no explanations, favorite food (and perhaps more importantly, least favorite food), colors, pets, and so on. These are the kinds of things professional helpers can use to bring their being with edgy youth to life, ensuring that they reflect the things on the young person's mind in their approach to being with them.

2. *What does s/he know about you?* Equally important as what the helper may know about the edgy youth is what the edgy youth knows about the helper. Indeed, this is something that is almost never considered in helping relationships, partly because, helpers are expected to maintain very firm boundaries around their clients in many settings and contexts, largely prohibiting self-disclosure. Yet it is difficult to imagine how a relationship between helper and young person can evolve and flourish when the young person remains ignorant about the humanity of the helper. Therefore, from the perspective of the professional helper, it is critical to ensure that the young person has opportunities to know things about him or her. Such things especially include those that impact the helper on a day to day basis, such as likes and dislikes in the areas of music, food, activities and sports. Furthermore, it also includes more fundamental aspects of the helper's life, including family context, professional context, personal hobbies and the like. This is important so that the young person is able to understand the everyday context of the professional helper, thereby

being able to see and experience the helper as a human being in his or her own right, rather than just as the ambassador of whatever helping system employs him or her.

3. *Times of day/night covered* – Being with edgy youth can be impacted by many different things, including the schedule when professional helpers and young people get together. Developmentally, young people can present very differently at different times of the day, and socially, the pressures of everyday life vary considerably as well. Being with edgy youth during the day may not provide the same opportunities for engagement and becoming connected to their peer groups and other aspects of the young person's life as being with them in the evening. Depending on the service settings, different times of the day provide for different program routines and expectations, and it is important for the professional helper to find a presence in all such contexts and routines, rather than only those that correspond to a steady day or evening schedule. Conversely, in order for edgy youth to allow for the professional helper to become present in their lives, they must experience his or her presence in multiple contexts, routines and experiences. This is more likely to happen when professional helpers consciously create schedules that cover a wide range of day and evening hours.

4. *Modes of communication* – as I have indicated earlier in this chapter, professional helpers must find ways of becoming present in the lives of edgy youth that transcend the limitations of face to face contact. This is not only the case in order to increase the time that the helpers are directly or actively engaged with the young person, but also to provide opportunities for the young person to utilize different modes of communication that may allow for different levels of conversation about particular topics. In some cases, for example, it may be difficult for an edgy youth to resolve a particular disagreement with the helper in person, but it may be entirely possible to do so over time through an exchange of a series of written notes. Very often, programs and services place unrealistic demands on edgy youth to resolve or come to terms with particular experiences or issues in their relationships, and when they are unable to meet those deadlines, their problem-solving skills, or even their social skills, are called into question. In fact, for many edgy youth, problem-solving and processing experiences with helpers and others simply take time, and rushing

them into accepting solutions to such problems may serve to increase their mistrust and misgivings about the helping system and the helper.

Therefore, professional helpers will significantly increase their presence in the lives of edgy youth by incorporating a range of communication modes, including e-mail where available, texting, social networking, written notes, telephone calls and gaming opportunities in their day to day communication with the youth. Although such a range of communication modes has implications for boundaries, professional helpers should still pursue all of these in the context of on-going negotiations about boundaries that fit the particular circumstances of their relationship with any given edgy youth.

5. *Whom do you know?* Far too often, professional helpers find themselves so focused on their interactions with edgy youth that they simply do not take the time or miss opportunities to meet in person, or by means of virtual technologies other important people in the life of the edgy youth. While incorporating family into professional work with edgy youth has become somewhat common place in most helping systems, there are still many other kinds of personal and social connections that are of great importance and that professional helpers ought to be connected to. This includes, perhaps most importantly, the peer group. Getting to know the friends and acquaintances of young people allows professional helpers to understand the everyday experiences of edgy youth much better. Moreover, this also allows the helpers to target their conversations in ways that might be of interest to the edgy youth. From the perspective of the edgy youth, professional helpers who have met their friends personally are much more present in their lives than those who comment on their friends (often in negative ways) and never having met them. Much of the real or imagined life of edgy youth unfolds in the context of peer relationships; therefore, it is critical for professional helpers to find their presence within those relationships.

Aside from peers, there are other people who might be important to edgy youth, and these could include other professionals such as police officers, probation workers, social workers or health care professionals, or they could include adults such as friends' parents, neighbors, extended family or others whom the young person frequently encounters. It is these relationships and everyday interactions of the edgy youth that make up the bulk of the young person's everyday experiences and routines. One cannot be present in the lives of edgy youth without connecting with those who are important from the perspective of the young person.

6. *Exposure to the mundane and the extraordinary* – perhaps it is because of their limited face to face contact with the edgy youth on their case loads that professional helpers often seek to achieve the extraordinary on each occasion that they see their client. Often, they plan extraordinary activities such as a trip to an amusement park, attendance at a show or a range of sporting activities. Although such attention to exposing edgy youth to extraordinary opportunities is well meaning and virtuous in many respects, it also has adverse effects in terms of becoming present in their life. In reality, most edgy youth spend considerable amounts of time doing not much of anything, and boredom, inactivity and a lack of extraordinary events characterizes most of their days. Therefore, it is important for professional helpers not to become associated with a presence only as it pertains to breaking these routines. Instead, professional helpers must find ways of becoming present in the ordinary, everyday context of edgy youth, even when this involves limited activity and seemingly no focus on particular goals or outcomes. Being with edgy youth is usually about exactly that: just being, rather than doing.

7. *Does the youth want to know about your edge?* Earlier I discussed the importance of edgy youth getting to know their professional helpers in ways that are similar to how the helpers get to know the youth. Beyond descriptors of preferences and dislikes, there is always the question about the more profound elements of the helper's personality and character and the extent to which the edgy youth ought to have access to this kind of more intimate knowledge about the helper. In other words, while the helper becomes very familiar with the young person's edge, does the young person become increasingly familiar with the helper's edge? It is likely that a meaningful approach to negotiating boundaries would place limits on the extent to which the young person might encounter the professional helper's edge. What is of greater interest is whether or not the young person continues to want to know about this edge. Helper-edgy youth relationships are most dynamic and interesting; therefore, also the most meaningful when there is on-going pressure on the negotiated boundaries and a need to continuously revisit such boundaries. While this does not mean that boundaries necessarily need to shift constantly, it does

mean that the preoccupation with boundaries becomes symptomatic of helper and edgy youth having found a significant mutual presence in their respective lives.

8. *Conflict with other parts of the service system* – Edgy youth are typically involved with multiple parts of the service systems, possibly including elements of mental health services, child protection services and youth justices services among others. Their experiences within all of these systems are rarely consistent, and while some such experiences may be positive, others may be negative, conflict-ridden or even traumatic. In these situations, professional helpers have opportunities to become present in the young person's experiences of other helping systems and settings in a variety of different roles, including: advocacy, support, mediator, negotiator, facilitator, and so on. It is important for professional helpers not to impose themselves in any of these roles, as this simply serves to leave the young person disempowered and to limit his or her ownership over these relationships and interactions. It is equally important, however, for the professional helper and the young person to create opportunities to jointly define a role for each in navigating some of the conflicts and experiences in others parts of the helping system. While the goal is not always to resolve conflict in this context, it at least ought to involve being present in these conflicts in ways that the young person can draw on the helper as a resource when needed, without having to give up his or her authority or ownership over the relationship or conflict.

9. *Ups and downs* – yet another measure of being present in the life of an edgy youth is the degree to which ups and downs are allowed to appear in the relationship between the helper and young person. Often, professional helpers work very hard to avoid downturns or setbacks in their relationships with young people; these are seen as obstacles to achieving treatment goals or imposing intervention strategies successfully. Building resistance on the part of the edgy youth is rarely recognized as an indication of presence, and, instead, is seen as being symptomatic of problems in the helper-youth relationship. In reality, very few relationships ever unfold without any ups and downs, and it is not the presence of ups and downs that defines a relationship; but instead the manner in which such ups and downs are managed and incorporated in the everyday presence of the helper in the life of the young person. The extent to which difficulties

and problems in the relationship come to define the evolution of the relationship speaks to the degree of presence the helper may have achieved in the life of the youth. A professional helper who has established himself or herself as present in most of the young person's everyday experiences, as discussed in the previous eight points, is not easily removed from that life; instead, youth and helper are forced to find ways of addressing downs that might be challenging and difficult for a period of time, but that ultimately confirm the strong presence of the helper in the life of the edgy youth.

10. *Absence trials* – a good way to measure the helper's presence in the life of the edgy youth is to practice absence for periods of time. This is a very difficult aspect of becoming present because most edgy youth have already had repeated experiences of abandonment and rejection in their lives. Therefore, it is critical that the practicing of absence is done in such a way that the edgy youth can still continue to seek out the helper's presence, such that that this presence increasingly becomes initiated by the young person, rather than the helper. Absence does not require complete severance of the relationship but simply a shift in how the presence is maintained. By ensuring that the onus for maintaining the presence of the helper gradually shifts to the edgy youth, opportunities are created for the edgy youth to seek out new relationships as these might become available without having to worry about responding to the presence of the professional helper. The helper remains responsive and highly engaged with the edgy youth but removes any pressure on the youth to respond in kind.

PRESENCE AND PERFORMANCE

What is perhaps most notable about the ten ways of becoming present in the lives of edgy youth is the complete absence of performance criteria imposed on the youth. Many traditional approaches of working with edgy youth impose such criteria, sometimes explicitly and sometimes in more nuanced ways. It is common, for example, for services to be goal oriented, whereby the goals pursued require the young person to take increasingly more difficult steps in the pursuit of a particular outcome. To the extent that these steps are taken and the outcomes are successfully reached, the presence of the professional helper takes on increasingly positive and reinforcing characteristics. When these steps are not taken and outcomes are not reached, the presence of the helper becomes imposing, blaming and judgmental. Indeed, performance expectations are often the foundation of the presence of the professional helper in the life of the edgy youth.

This approach reflects the formalities and the focus on logistical considerations of helping systems, often in very subtle ways. Edgy youth are made to conform to the time lines for growth and change imposed by the system, and their success or failure in so doing determine the actions of the system. Presence, I argue, cannot be made to depend on the performance of edgy youth in relation to imposed expectations. Such presence is greeted with suspicion on the part of the youth and most often becomes compartmentalized as an intervention in their everyday life. The goal of being with edgy youth is not to intervene in their everyday life, but to provide guidance and support to them by directing their everyday life in ways that are meaningful and productive from the perspective of the youth as well as the professional helper and society-at-large.

In this chapter, I have argued that becoming present is the foundation of being with edgy youth. Not much useful change can happen for edgy youth if professional helpers fail to develop a presence in their lives that is comprehensive, far-reaching and that touches all of the complexity of their physical, mental, virtual and relational spaces. Becoming present in this way requires that professional helpers recognize the central roles of the youth in determining the path of presence that presents itself within the helper-youth relationship.

Chapter 5

STAY WITH IT!

The most difficult thing about being with edgy youth is that whatever we might imagine we are contributing to the young person's life is not likely to yield measurable outcomes for a long time. In fact, it is quite likely that being with edgy youth is going to be frustrating. At times, the young person will appear to be making progress in directions that we approve of, and at other times, the young person will be sliding backwards and intensifying the very behaviors and actions that were the reason for our involvement in the first place. Being with edgy youth is not a straight forward activity, and it certainly is not one that is satisfying and rewarding because of the impact we are having on the young person. No matter how brilliant a professional helper may be, and no matter how committed and democratic and wonderful the engagement of the youth might be, being with edgy youth is going to be rocky, unpredictable, sometimes very frustrating and even disappointing, and often times simply unbelievable. And still, my message to professional helpers, their helping systems and society at large is simply this: Stay with it!

Edgy youth do not make it easy to stay with them. In spite of our efforts to get over it, not to personalize and to become present, edgy youth often repay us by being extremely anti-social, completely ungrateful and even criminal and violent, if not against us, then at least against some other innocent victim in the community. As a result, it is not surprising that we often reach a point of wanting to quit; not our jobs, but rather our efforts to hang in there with particular young people who have pushed our limits of acceptance and tolerance beyond what we can take. When this happens, our compassion, our empathy and our caring are replaced very quickly, decisively and absolutely by a desire to punish and to exclude. This is when we return to clear solutions such as incarceration, secure treatment or outright service refusals for older youth. We say to ourselves and each other "We have tried everything, and clearly this young person is beyond repair. It is time to get serious and protect the community and himself from his actions, from his poor choices, from his violence."

On the surface, this seems reasonable enough. In those cases where we give up on young people we can usually document our efforts well. We can show the efforts we have made, the price we have paid, and the risks we have taken. It is almost never the case that we, including any professional helper and the various helping systems in the community, simply gave up on a young person without trying. Furthermore, in virtually every case where we have given up on a young person, we can tell stories about that young person's actions that are scary. These are stories of increasing violence, abuse of peers and adults, serious criminal activity, gang involvement, sexual assaults, drug use, arson and a host of other anti-social and dangerous activities. Under the circumstances, can anyone really blame us for finally giving up?

The answer to this seemingly rhetorical question is a resounding, "Yes!" We can be blamed, and indeed we must be blamed for these kinds of outcomes. In the end, a fundamental principle cannot be violated, no matter what the circumstances, the stories or the dangers surrounding a particular young person: no one is left behind. Rationalizing why it might be alright to throw out a young person's life and take no further interest in it or responsibility for it is not an option; it is symptomatic of the decay in societal values, reflecting our preoccupation with creating easy and ready-made solutions to enduring social problems. There are at least four reasons why failing to stay with it when it comes to being with edgy youth reflects a serious error in thinking on the part of professional helpers and their helping systems. Some of these reasons also reflect the shortsightedness of societal expectations when it comes to maintaining law and order as well as community safety. I want to explore each of these reasons below.

SIMPLE MISTAKES

When young people appear to be embarking on a path of self-destruction and ever escalating anti-social behavior, one gets the impression that they were doomed from the beginning anyway, and that it is not so much that our interventions along the way were wrong or inappropriate, but rather that there is some genetic, chemical or biological reason for why this young person is damaged beyond repair. Professional helping systems take great comfort in these kinds of rationalizations. Although it is not usually intended this way, blaming youth for their failures continues to be a common practice in the helping professions. Our language may have changed somewhat and we certainly have made huge gains in terms of developing the necessary range of psychiatric diagnoses to label these lost young people, but fundamentally we continue to look to the youth to either reverse course or to live with their chronic failure and lack of capacity to turn things around.

From the perspective of edgy youth, an entirely different story emerges. This is a story about being misunderstood, treated badly, ignored, disempowered, ridiculed, not listened to and fundamentally marginalized in their journey toward growth and personal fulfillment. If one listens carefully enough, it becomes readily apparent that these young people can identify specific occasions and particular events where decisions were made or actions were taken that pushed them one step further down the road of becoming "irreversibly" lost. Whether it was the abuse suffered at the hands of a family member or being ignored at a moment of need by a professional helper in a residential care program, edgy youth incorporate these experiences in their overall experience with the world and everyone in it. As it turns out, edgy youth embarking on the path of self destruction and anti-social behavior can identify literally hundreds of such moments where whatever they believed to be true and worthy was struck down abruptly by deceit, ignorance or a dismissive gesture.

Simple mistakes in the interactions between professional helpers and edgy youth happen because for the professional helpers and their helping systems, each youth is like every other. As a result, these systems present young people with processes and procedures that all function the same way, hold the same expectations and produce the same outcomes regardless of the uniqueness or the unique circumstances of a particular youth. Intake processes, for example, are virtually always universally structured so that every young person in need of service will have to accept an identical process to become eligible to receive that service. Young people who resist this and insist on being treated as an individual often pay the price for their demands. Professional helpers rarely have the patience and the skills to individualize, customize or personalize services that are structured in such a way that consistency and routine govern their implementation. From the perspective of the edgy youth, on the other hand, virtually all interactions with professional helpers and their helping systems are extremely personal and are remembered as such. To the extent that edgy youth sense a rejection on the part of the professional helper or the helping system, even if this is based strictly on logistical and bureaucratic processes, their openness and preparedness to engage the helper and the helping system is impacted. Over time, an accumulation of events and experiences that appear to confirm the rejection of the young person's individuality pushes the young person to simply move on and to respond to this rejection with his or her own rejection of being helped.

In this sense, edgy youth who appear to be choosing the path of self-destruction and anti-social behavior are not making such choices randomly or without context. Quite to the contrary, they are responding to their experiences of rejection or feeling uncared for based on very specific actions on the part of professional helpers. As a result, we maintain an enormous responsibility to stay with these youth who are rapidly moving away from us because they are doing so in response to our mistakes. In this sense, we can indeed blame ourselves for these young people getting lost, but rather than spending time and energy on blaming ourselves, we ought to carefully listen to these young people so that we can avoid making simple mistakes as we re-engage them and re-commit ourselves to staying with it.

ON-GOING LEARNING

An interesting but rarely acknowledged dynamic in service provision for marginalized or at-risk populations is that the programs and services developed virtually never end up meeting the needs of the entire target population. Instead, no matter what the target group for a particular service might be, the service will inevitably serve only the most competent within that target group. Although the services will be offered to members of the target group who appear to be stuck in whatever their situation might be, these members of the target group are generally seen as largely inconsequential since they do not get in the way of the most competent members of the target group. Quite predictably, however, there is virtually always a group within the target population, typically consisting of about 10% of the total target population, that not only fails to benefit from the services offered, but that appears to get worse. To make matters even worse, this sub-group of the target group often is seen as a distraction to the rest of the target group, and very often this sub-group becomes targeted by professional helpers and their helping systems as candidates for exclusion. Below I will refer to this sub-group of the target group as "the bottom 10%". This term is not to label this group as unworthy or as less valuable than the remainder of the target group, but it is to highlight the often dismissive manner in which this group is treated.

A common scenario adversely affecting edgy youth is that of the shelter system designed to provide emergency housing for street-involved young people. Virtually all youth shelters aim to provide emergency housing and other basic needs assistance to young people on the streets in ways that are inclusive to everyone affected. Over time, however, professional helpers employed in the shelter notice that some of the youth appear to be making some progress to resolve whatever their cause of street involvement might have been, or alternatively to find housing and employment and, therefore, sustainably move off the streets. The same professional helpers also notice, however, that there is a group of youth who seem to involve themselves in the business of the young people who are serious about improving their situation, and, frequently, this second group of youth actually comes in the way of the first group of serious young people succeeding. In response, the professional helpers begin to plot against this second group of youth and before anyone really notices what has happened, the second group of youth is discharged from the shelter for being disruptive and unhelpful in the shelter's attempt to help street involved youth get off the streets. The surprising outcome is that the very system designed to help young people stay off the streets now has forced a group of young people to return to the streets. Somehow the mandate of being inclusive and rejecting no one has been sidelined, ostensibly for virtuous reasons but essentially in violation of the very raison d'être of the shelter.

This dynamic of excluding the bottom 10% of young people in any given service or program has existed for many years, and somehow we have become quite comfortable with accepting this. Whether it is in the homelessness system or in residential care and treatment, in education or in community-based recreation programs, we appear to have become quite complacent toward our failure to meet the needs of a group of young people who are deemed less responsive to our attempts to serve them than others. What is interesting, however, is that this group of 10% is always present, meaning that once we abandon the first group of 10%, a second such group will form among those who remain in the program or service.

We must begin to deal with the reality that we will never have a group of young people in any helping service where every member of the group responds in the same manner, generally positively and always attentively to the programs and services offered. So long as we simply continue to eliminate those young people who cannot keep up with the performance of the other, more successful, young people, we will learn absolutely nothing about how to be with edgy youth. What we will perfect, over time, is our capacity to render conformist and compliant the majority of young people in the program at the expense of the group of 10%. If we continuously eliminate the young people who challenge our ways of providing services and structuring programs, why would we ever try to do things differently? Indeed, this approach, characterized by serving only the performing young people, fundamentally negates the very purpose of having helping systems in the first place. One might argue that this purpose is to be present with those who cannot do it in the settings or social contexts that are provided for them and who, therefore, need us to be with them as they fight their way toward personal growth and fulfillment. Instead, we are structurally embedding a group of the bottom 10% in the helping systems, and we are ethically legitimizing their abandonment. I would argue that this is unacceptable and, therefore, another reason to always stay with it.

THE CONSEQUENCE OF ABANDONMENT

It may seem like it is not such a big deal to occasionally abandon a young person, especially after we have tried everything we could think of to help that young person move from the edge to the center. The economics of social complacency are pretty simple: if we help most of the kids conform to societal expectations, losing a few along the way is not a catastrophe. Sometimes one has to face facts and accept that some young people simply cannot make it in our society. But what are the consequences of this kind of economics?

First, it is worthwhile to ask the most obvious question with respect to the young people that we decide to abandon: where do they go? Many edgy youth spend a little time in custodial facilities, and as they move into adulthood, probably also in jails. While there, they meet other edgy youth who, like them, feel rejected and have been abandoned by the helping systems in their lives. Their conversations are not likely to be about the good times they have had in life. In fact, what they are most likely to talk about is what they will do when they get out, who they will exact revenge from, who will pay for their mistakes, and how they might make a living in the absence of a job or anyone financially supporting them. In other words, most edgy youth who find themselves spending time in jail for whatever sort of crime will leave jail as a better prepared, better connected and fired up criminal.

It is important to understand the dynamics we create when we choose to abandon young people to their own devices. For one thing, we create edgy youth whose social contacts and personal connections are likely to be limited to other edgy youth. Wherever they turn, they find only more of what they already have or a greater need for what they lack. Their friends and acquaintances are angry, lonely, and ready to snap at any time. These social groups are connected to gangs, drugs and violent crime. Recruiting for these social groups is made easy when we add to their social scene edgy youth fresh from being rejected and abandoned, even by the very people whose professional existence is largely dependent on there being edgy youth in our neighborhoods to begin with. But it doesn't stop there. In fact, edgy youth crave emotional connections, love, intimacy and all the other human feelings and needs associated with emerging adulthood. They are sexual beings as well, and, not surprisingly, they find only each other for the purpose of intimate and sexual relationships. Edgy youth, for better or for worse, have a long standing pattern of recreating themselves. Young parenthood is common, with girls giving birth, sometimes to fill a significant void in their loveless lives and other times as the outcome of sexual violence that is common but rarely reported in this social group.

It comes as no surprise that the consequences of abandonment are dire for the edgy youth; but they are also significant for professional helpers, their helping systems and society at large. Most of the time, we find these abandoned edgy youth in central areas of our communities, and very often we reject not only the youth but even the places where they gather. Indeed, middle class values and sensibilities result in parents warning their children about interacting with these edgy youth, making physical detours to avoid confrontation (such as exchanging greetings) with the young people, and registering complaints to police and city officials about their loitering habits and profane language. In perhaps only slightly nuanced ways, our abandonment of these edgy youth results in a class system in which the youth are clearly at the bottom of a wealth and value-based social hierarchy. To make matters worse, we allow this situation to absorb a range of issues that are clearly otherwise broader social issues of everyone's concerns. Edgy youth become not only associated with criminality, mental health problems and anti-social behaviors, but they are labeled as the perpetrators of crime, mental health and an anti-social existence that feeds on free loading and violence.

As a result of these dynamics, societies begin to take shape in directions that surely were unanticipated when we abandoned the bottom 10% youth in our programs and services designed to be helpful to them. What we are left with are neighborhoods and communities that are blinded by their unfounded phobia of edgy youth. Never mind that most violent crimes in Canada, the US and much of Europe is perpetrated by adult men against women; if anyone is attacked in the neighborhood, an edgy youth must be to blame. Never mind that mental health concerns are prevalent in all social groups, and especially among professionals where nearly 30% are thought to suffer from depression; it is edgy youth who are all crazy and in need of containment. In fact, what we create by abandoning edgy youth who appear to be getting lost are communities and neighborhoods that are divided, where fear reigns supreme and where we once again are prepared to accept blatant forms of discrimination and social marginalization based on membership in a particular social group. This surely cannot be the goal of any helping professional or their helping systems. What we ought to be working towards is not the abandonment of edgy youth when we no longer know what to do with them, but instead a restoration of neighborhood and community health when our young people seem to feel rejected and marginalized within these, and alienated and excluded from these.[1]

SOCIO-DEGRADABLE VIOLENCE?

One of the reasons we find ourselves pushed to abandon young people is because we simply cannot stand the violence. At any rate, putting an end to the violence seems like the responsible thing to do. Time and time again professional helpers and their helping systems do what they can to avoid abandoning edgy youth, but when it does happen, it almost invariably has something to do with the young person's use of violence against peers, professional helpers and sometimes even themselves. In an effort to protect others, to keep neighborhoods safe and sometimes to protect themselves, professional helpers legitimize the abandonment of edgy youth on the basis that this will eliminate violence. But will it really? Can violence be eliminated?

The answer is, of course, that it cannot be eliminated. Violence is neither biodegradable nor socio-degradable. Once it has been unleashed, it will exist forever, even if its form and impact do change over time. Ignoring this violence is hardly a progressive move, and certainly will do nothing to make the world a safer place. Abandoning edgy youth who have been violent may

---

[1] This is the premise of the restorative justice movement that advocates for healing circles and other means of resolving conflict and restoring health in schools, neighborhoods and communities. Research has demonstrated that restorative justice approaches are extraordinarily successful in producing sustainable outcomes related to conflict-resolution. See for example Bazemore & Schiff (2005) and also Hayden & Gough (2010).

reduce the risk of overt forms of violence in a particular program or service in the immediate term, but the roots of violence have already been firmly planted, ready to sprout once the next young person decides to take on its cause.

Victims of violence do not simply get over their victimizations once the perpetrator has been punished. In fact, the memory and the eerie feeling of being violated are ever present once violence has reared its ugly head. Most programs and services for young people are marked by violence in many different forms. They experience the violent outbursts on the part of some of the youth, but they also experience the violent response, even if legalized and regulated, on the part of the professional helpers who might intervene with physical containment strategies. Much of the everyday violence that unfolds in programs and services, and especially in custodial services, goes unnoticed by the professional helpers, and new victims of violence are created with each passing day (Finlay, 2005). In this kind of context, eliminating violence by rejecting and abandoning a young person caught in the act of violence is a form of violence. It is symptomatic of lashing out, of striking down those who can easily be struck down, with the striker protected by the legitimizing discourse of, "We did what we could, but we have to keep the others safe."

Instead of abandoning those who have touched the violence, either by perpetrating it or by promoting it, professional helpers and their helping systems must learn to engage this violence; it will never go away. We cannot purify the physical settings where professional helpers work and pretend that no violence is ever perpetrated there. We are far better at accepting this violence as part of the experience of being with edgy youth, by vigorously challenging it every day by exposing it, by labeling it and by fighting it in a transparent and engaged way, rather than through abandonment and rejection. Sticking with the violent young people ensures that their violence will be confronted. Abandoning these young people ensures that their violence can continue to unfold unchecked, even if from time to time it unfolds in custodial or jail facilities.

These are four reasons why abandoning edgy youth is not a good move. Doing so will destroy the young people for good, but it also lessens the value of the professional helper and their helping systems. In some respects, one might argue that the helping systems' chronic inability to engage the bottom 10% of youth in their programs and services is quite an admission of failure. Why should any of the helping professions be elevated in social status and material compensation when all that they can do is to engage those among their client groups who are quite obviously easily engaged? In reality, it is not merely for the sake of the edgy youth that we ought not to abandon them.

Professional helpers seeking to be recognized for their unique skills and professional fields need to find ways of being with edgy youth in order to confirm their value to society at large. After all, *containing* edgy youth does not require professional helpers; if that really were the task at hand, security guards, or even remotely monitored physical structures would do just fine.

Professional helpers want more than simply doing what they can before being pushed to abandon the young people. I remain convinced that the overwhelming majority of professional helpers is actively searching for a different way of being with edgy youth; one that will allow them to continue to be present and engaged, even if some measures related to safety and accountability must be taken. Most professional helpers know that abandonment is not the answer and sticking with it, in the face of enormous challenges, is possible and must happen. One of the first steps they must take in order to build a strong foundation for sticking with it is to understand and respect young people's perspectives on being with professional helpers. As it turns out, these perspectives are often much more complex than first thought.

YOU ARE NOT MY PARENT!

For edgy youth, a professional helper is somewhat of an enigma. On the one hand, the youth are fully aware that a professional helper is present in their lives as part of their job obligations and that these helpers get paid to be present in their lives. On the other hand, the youth also sense that there is a level of commitment embedded in the way in which professional helpers become present in their lives that cannot be explained solely on the basis of their earnings. This makes it difficult to conceptualize the role of a professional helper in terms of more familiar categories. Edgy youth might consider such helpers to be friends, extended family, and even proxy parents. At the same time, the youth are aware that whatever role their specific helper might assume, or whatever role the youth might bestow on the helper, that role is ultimately time limited and contingent on the continued association of the young person and the programs and services where the helper works. Unlike extended family and parents, the involvement of professional helpers in the lives of edgy youth is specific to time, place and context, and it is not easily transferred across time, place and context. Moreover, whereas extended family and parents can autonomously determine the intensity and the parameters of their involvement in the lives of the young person, professional helpers cannot often do this; they must remain accountable to the requirements of their jobs and the policies and procedures of their specific assignments.

From the perspective of edgy youth, therefore, the role of professional helpers shifts considerably as time passes, and although it is not always possible for the youth to identify what the role of a professional helper is, it is quite possible to identify what it is not. Edgy youth almost invariably come to the conclusion that their professional helper, even under the best possible circumstances, is not their friend, their extended family or their parent. Indeed, the relationship with the professional helper is more closely tied to the association with the program or service that employs the helper, rather than with the everyday experiences of the edgy youth.

The implications of this perspective on the part of edgy youth are important for professional helpers to consider. When edgy youth begin to disassociate from programs and services the relationship with the professional helper is also impacted, and the helper then faces the dilemma of either insisting that the young person re-commit to the program or finding ways of re-connecting, or re-contextualizing the connection with the young person outside of the parameters of the program. Either of these approaches is difficult to implement. In the first case, the attempt to have the young person stick with the program or service inevitably becomes a matter of persuasion, backed by control and authority. It will not take long before the professional helper, previously well connected to the young person, begins to sound very much like the pre-packaged messages of the program. The more that the young person resists those messages, the more these elements of control and authority will creep into the interactions between the helper and the young person. In the second case, however, re-contextualizing the professional helper's presence in the life of the edgy youth outside of the parameters of the program requires some element of managerial support for maintaining such connections. Perhaps more importantly, this will also require that the professional helper find some substantive content for his or her on-going connection with the young person, without the assistance of program structures and routines. This, it turns out, can be more difficult than might appear at first glance.

What is necessary, then, is for the professional helper to learn the art of "being", rather than the skills involved in "doing". Sticking with it is not ultimately a function of doing anything in particular, because the challenges associated with sticking with it are primarily challenges related to the actions of the edgy youth.

In most frameworks for intervention, the goal is described as changing the behavior, or the actions of the edgy youth, so as to bring them back to a place where conformity and compliance at least seem possible. What I am proposing is that the necessary intervention for sticking with it is learning not to do anything at all, and instead discovering the art of being present with edgy youth as they accumulate some very difficult and possibly life-altering experiences. When edgy youth begin to disassociate from the professional helpers and their helping systems and move toward increasingly edgy life styles and decision-making, they are without a doubt exposed to considerable risks to their personal safety as well as to their future opportunities. While it may seem urgent to mitigate these risks, what is more urgent is to avoid another problem that can act as a catalyst for complete implosion on the part of the edgy youth; this is the problem of loss. After all, disassociating from programs and services puts edgy youth in a position of having to reconstitute an entirely new set of structures and routines for their everyday life. This is hard enough, but losing important relationships at the same time might make it impossible to do so. Sticking with it, therefore, provides edgy youth with a reference point, a place of stability that doesn't place demands on them to conform or comply, but that provides opportunities for them to regulate the range of their high risk behaviors and decisions.

In the next section of this chapter, I want to explore four core elements of being with edgy youth that will help professional helpers assume this all-important role in the lives of edgy youth. Specifically, these are four characteristics of being with edgy youth that provide opportunities for the youth to self-regulate as they move beyond the helping systems' capacities to control what happens next. These four characteristics are the offer of silence, the place of wisdom, the depository of dreams and the place of reliable honesty. I will describe each of these below.

THE OFFER OF SILENCE

The lives of edgy youth are typically very turbulent. This is true of their lives before they receive services from helping professionals but it remains true, and sometimes becomes even truer, once they start receiving such services. This is a weakness in how services are provided to edgy youth. A great deal of activity takes place from the start as professional helping systems absorb the very soul of the edgy youth into their machineries. From bureaucratic processes to logistical requirements and from clinical interventions to case meetings and the establishment of plans of care, there is invariably a lot of "noise" involved in being with edgy youth within the context of traditional programs and services. The activities of edgy youth while receiving such services and participating in programs are closely monitored; their behavior is analyzed and interpreted and clinical labels are suggested, dismissed or assigned. Although there are moments where edgy youth do get to have a voice in these processes, and in spite of recent improvements in attempts at youth engagement activities on the part of many helping systems, ultimately much of what edgy youth experience in their interactions with helping systems is noise.

Professional helpers are trained to try and help young people make sense of their own lives. Much of the noise that is being generated is really designed to facilitate this process of self-exploration and discovery. It is also a process that is pre-loaded with permissible paths and areas of self-exploration. Deviations from this path, once again, raise the volume of intervention, and edgy youth quickly learn that if they want to avoid such noise it is best to disengage with the helping systems as much as possible. This is one of the limitations facing professional helpers who understand that edgy youth want to escape the noise of the helping system. They are forced by their job descriptions to pull the young people back from a path of self-exploration that deviates from what has been prescribed by the service or the program. In this way, edgy youth never really get to move far enough along their path of self discovery to learn anything. What they must do instead is to completely sever their association with the helping systems in order to really be able to pursue their own path.

From the perspective of professional helpers, it is very difficult to observe edgy youth embarking on a journey of risk and likely mistakes that will cost them dearly. They have already worked hard to stabilize these young people and to develop some meaningful routines and structure in their lives; letting go of them now is something professional helpers find enormously difficult. In most cases, their attempts at reigning in the edgy youth will fail, and then all that is left is to give up. What rarely is considered as an option is to continue the commitment to being with edgy youth through the offer of silence, rather than noise.

Silence is invaluable to edgy youth and often something that they have never been able to experience for very long in their young lives. Silence consists of the presence of someone of importance in the life of the edgy youth without the intervention that usually accompanies this presence. A professional helper can offer silence to an edgy youth by being present, but by avoiding active intervention or even the offer to assist in resolving a particular problem or situation. The helper is there to render the young person's self-exploration less lonely, more connected to the outside world and ultimately just a little more comfortable knowing that there is the opportunity to tell the story to someone who will listen to it. Furthermore, the offer of silence is characterized by complete non-judgment and a lack of expectations with respect to outcomes. In other words, the professional helper neither confirms nor denies the possibilities for negative outcomes, but simply offers his or her presence in the life of the edgy youth as these outcomes become apparent. When the outcome is positive, the helper is present without celebration; when the outcome is negative, the helper remains present without imposing consequences. Ownership of the outcomes of the edgy youth's decisions is entirely devolved to the edgy youth, and the professional helper's role is to acknowledge and accept the young person in the context of whatever outcomes might be emerging.

Lest one get the impression that the offer of silence is an easy thing to do, or reflects a way of avoiding one's responsibilities to intervene when edgy youth appear to be making poor decisions, it is important to note that this offer of silence follows years of noise impositions. In other words, the professional helper is offering this silence in order to avoid the negative outcomes that have already been demonstrated in response to the noise of intervention; it is *because of this noise* the young person had to embark on his own journey of self-exploration. Remaining silent in the face of elevated risks and clearly unhelpful decisions on the part of the young person is very difficult for professional helpers. Helpers are trained to mitigate risks, to intervene in the face of poor decision-making and to seek control over what happens next. Offering silence, therefore, means that professional helpers have to offer their presence by actively suppressing their impulse to intervene and to act. For the first time in many cases, professional helpers have to work hard to live the principles they preach: non-judgment, youth empowerment, acknowledgment of the young person's unique approach to life, personal growth and development. Doing nothing, it turns out, is often much more difficult than doing something. Nevertheless, doing nothing is also often less destructive than doing something and being with edgy youth cannot always be about healing and fixing the young person; sometimes, it is simply about being present.

From the perspective of edgy youth, having the professional helper present through silence is an extraordinary gift. Edgy youth feel very lonely and abandoned when they finally do choose to embark on their own journey, and yet they cannot get unstuck from the control of helping systems without taking this leap. Therefore, the silent presence of their helper is precisely the kind of safe haven and emotional crutch they need. Over time, edgy youth learn that their silent professional helper can be more than just silently present. Without turning to interventions and the imposition of values reflective of the helping systems, the professional helper can provide something that is of enormous value to edgy youth: wisdom.

A PLACE OF WISDOM

Professional helpers are trained to provide interventions because it is through interventions that the pace of change, growth and personal development can be manipulated. The ability to manipulate the pace of change is considered important in helping systems because these systems are constructed around logistical and bureaucratic needs and usually provide for only limited time exposure to edgy youth. Professional helpers can provide something other than interventions that is of great value to edgy youth who spend much of their days in the here and now, slugging it out with peers against a multitude of challenges and adversity. Disconnected from interventions and advice on how to do things or how to avoid problems, professional helpers can represent a place of wisdom for edgy youth, where complex thoughts and feelings can be translated into meaningful and memorable narratives and sound bites.

The reality is that edgy youth are confronted with very difficult social, emotional and material dilemmas almost daily, and resolving such dilemmas is not easy. External advice on what to do is almost always unhelpful in these situations, since such advice is often far too disassociated from the identity of the young person and the specific circumstances confronting him or her. What the edgy youth are really seeking in these situations is a meaningful frame of reference that combines moral considerations with the more pragmatic considerations related to gratification, benefit to self and others, and possible expansion of future opportunities. In everyday life, such frames of references are difficult to come by, in part because there is not much wisdom out there that is reflective of independent thinking. Most of what is offered as wisdom by either peers or other helping professionals is tied to the personal ambitions or organizational value systems of those who offer this wisdom. Professional helpers who have already established their offer of silence are well-positioned to transcend these suspicions about their wisdom. In conjunction with the silence being offered, their wisdom reflects thoughts and philosophical musings about particular circumstances and situations. The young person is at liberty to do as he or she sees fit with these musing.

By way of example, we can imagine an edgy youth struggling with the idea of reconnecting with family. Advice from peers and other professionals is typically framed in very black or white terms: "You should try to reconnect," or "don't waste your time." Professional helpers who are already connected to the young person, and who have proven their commitment through the offer of silence, can, when asked, offer wisdom that is meaningful to the specific young person facing this situation: "Given everything that has happened, re-connecting will be hard and painful, but being connected to family is a wonderful thing." Such non-directive wisdom is articulated simply enough to be understandable to the young person while not imposing a particular course of action. A realistic representation of process and outcome is offered. Weighing the costs and benefits of embarking on the process in order to achieve the outcome is up to the young person. Moreover, this kind of wisdom allows the young person to also think about timing. Instead of moving ahead when he or she might not be ready, or dismissing the possibility of reunifications all together, the young person can maintain a neutral position and revisit this dilemma when the timing seems better.

Having access to non-threatening wisdom is very important for edgy youth. Given all of the social and emotional pressures facing these young people every day, making sense of the full complexity of life on the edge can be challenging. Professional helpers who are sticking with the young person beyond the young person's disassociation from the formal services and programs can offer up this kind of wisdom at a time when no one else can do so, unencumbered by program or service expectations or competitive interests typical within peer groups.

The offer of silence and the place of wisdom, together, provide the foundation for a trusting and meaningful relationship between professional helper and young person that can unfold in a context of informality and outside of specific service goals. Nevertheless, both of these elements of being with edgy youth are responses to the needs and issues of edgy youth in the here and now. A third element of being with edgy youth provides opportunities to meet an entirely different need of the youth; this is the depository of dreams, ensuring that edgy youth can live their lives right here and now yet still maintain a foothold in a future of their own construction.

THE DEPOSITORY OF DREAMS

In spite of the enormous challenges and adversity they face every day, edgy youth are often some of the most optimistic young people around. They have high hopes for the future and construct elaborate schemes of where they will be and what their lives might eventually look like. Although they don't always have a clear vision of how to achieve their hopes and dreams, they nevertheless hang on to these as important elements of their identity. These dreams are what help many edgy youth make it through the day. During the long and silent moments of loneliness, dreaming about what might be in the future is one way of maintaining one's inspiration for life.

A challenge faced by edgy youth is sharing these dreams with others. Very often others, and especially professional helpers and their helping systems, have very muted responses to such dreams and aspirations. Instead of celebrating and safeguarding the dream, they tend to reframe and downsize it, trying to instill some current reality into how the dream fits with the young person's perceived capacities. As a result, the dreams of edgy youth are always at risk and struggle to find a safe home. Particularly as edgy youth embark on some more rocky roads of self-exploration and discovery and in the process accumulate some challenging experiences that may include substance use, jail time, and other "failures", their dreams are at risk of being dismissed altogether as fairy tales and useless fantasies.

One element of sticking with it is associated with the safeguarding of the dreams of edgy youth. Therefore, professional helpers who know about the importance of sticking with it accept the depository of dreams as one of their roles during the difficult times in being with edgy youth. In this role, professional helpers maintain their accessibility to the edgy youth to deposit either their long standing dreams for safeguarding or to deposit new dreams or revisions to older dreams without any sort of judgmental response or dismissive commentary. The professional helper accepts the dreams as presented and declares his or her preparedness to safeguard these over longer periods of time, so that the young person can move along managing the day to day priorities without having to conjure up old or new dreams that might otherwise be forgotten. This is an enormously important function for the professional helper, allowing the young person to maintain a safety net that is forward looking and future-oriented. Edgy youth are always at risk of losing their future-orientation and being reduced to living only in the present. When this happens, the burden of living on the edge can easily become overwhelming, and each day blends into the next without any distinctions.

Knowing that their dreams are safely guarded by the professional helper, however, allows edgy youth to access the future whenever they can or whenever they feel ready to do so. While not much progress toward achieving a particular dream may be made for long periods of time, owning that dream, in spite of on-going challenges and potentially moving further away from making the dream a reality, is indicative of personal growth and development. The dream provides a reference point that is stable and predictable, and edgy youth can orient themselves toward their dream, even as their material and everyday living circumstances are constantly changing.

It is important for professional helpers to understand that it is immaterial whether or not edgy youth ever access their dreams once they are deposited with the helper. It is the fact that the dream exists and is safe that matters, not whether or not the young person is getting closer to achieving it. Being with edgy youth is less about the observable and measurable changes that happen and more about the possibility of change based on hopes, dreams and aspirations. The richness of the human experience is found in the striving toward something more so than in achieving it. This is especially true for edgy youth, many of whom use the process of striving toward something as their structure in life, given the absence of other more formal structures such as schools, jobs, family or community involvement. Acting as the depository of dreams provides a link between the present and the future, maintained jointly by the professional helper and the edgy youth. Much like the Offer of Silence and the Place of Wisdom, this component of being with edgy youth is still relatively passive and provides opportunities for the young person to self-direct his or her self-exploration and journey of discovery. The fourth and final element of being with edgy youth pushes us to think beyond this concrete representation of passivity and explore the more ambiguous space of passive intervention. This is the Place of Reliable Honesty.

THE PLACE OF RELIABLE HONESTY

No matter how we might approach our commitment to sticking with it and to being with edgy youth who are embarking on their high risk and often turbulent journey of self-exploration and discovery, we will always struggle with remaining silent in the face of what we believe to be poor choices and potentially life altering risks and safety concerns. On the one hand, we recognize the importance of the offering of silence, as I discussed above. On the other hand, we wish to maintain a level of integrity in our interactions with the edgy youth that reflects values such as honesty, transparency, reliability and commitment. The time will come when the reassertion of these values takes precedent over our protective and nurturing stance toward the young person's journey of self-exploration and discovery. Especially when it comes to being honest, edgy youth need to know that they can rely on their professional helpers to consistently and directly deliver honest feedback.

Therefore, sticking with it requires that professional helpers assume the role of being a place of reliable honesty for edgy youth. Honesty is not always gentle and kind, but it always delivers a message that is important enough to cause someone to pause and reflect. This is a core goal of professional helpers in their interactions with edgy youth. Meaningful reflections on the part of edgy youth, concerning their own actions and decisions, cannot happen in the absence of honest feedback from someone close enough to understand the context of such actions and decisions. Sometimes this feedback needs to be personal and direct. This means that the professional helper engages the young person not only in relation to what the young person is doing, but also in relation to how the actions of the young person impact on the helper. "I don't like what you are doing," is an honest and direct response to the young person that needs to be openly expressed. Note the distinction between this statement and a statement that seeks to prejudge outcomes: "This will not work out well." This latter statement is not reflective of reliable honesty: it prejudges something based on probabilities and a subjective judgment of context. The underlying message is that based on what the helper knows of the young person, the young person's demonstrated record in related matters and the overall likelihood of being successful in relation to whatever action the young person is contemplating, the helper does not believe the desired result will be obtained. Such statements are not about honesty, but rather are challenges to the young person to prove the helper wrong. "I don't like what you are doing," in contrast, is an absolute truth, one that cannot be contested by anyone inasmuch as only the helper can speak to what he or she may or may not like. This statement neither encourages the young person to proceed nor explicitly discourages the young person from proceeding. Instead, it provides important information about how the actions of the young person are impacting someone who has been with the young person in many important ways and through some very difficult times. It is still up to the edgy youth to decide how much weight to place on the fact that the helper does not like his or her actions.

Edgy youth are always interested in feedback about what they are doing or contemplating doing. The difficulty is that they often do not have people in their lives whose feedback is sufficiently neutral yet also informed in relation to their everyday lives. Professional helpers who stick with it, even when edgy youth begin to disassociate from the formal helping systems, can fill this void and can provide that feedback. The value of this feedback is maintained only when it is reliably honest, no matter how difficult it might be at times to be honest. Like all young people, edgy youth prefer to receive positive and confirming feedback about their actions and their intentions. Consequently, delivering negative feedback can result in hard feelings and momentary tension in relationships. Nonetheless, it is vital that the youth can rely on the professional helper to always deliver the message in its truest form. Only then does becoming a Place of Reliable Honesty complement the long term commitment to being with edgy youth.

BEING WITH, NOT BEING AN, EDGY YOUTH

In this final section of this chapter, I want to make a point that might appear obvious and redundant, but that, in fact, reflects a crucial distinction in thinking about being with edgy youth. This is the distinction between being with edgy youth on the one hand, and attempting to be like an edgy youth on the other hand. Professional helpers are always concerned about the degree to which edgy youth can relate to them or believe that they can relate to edgy youth. For these reasons, even agencies and organizations that work with edgy youth often develop what amount to discriminatory hiring practices that privilege youth over experience. Helpers who are thought to be too old to relate to teenage cultures, or whom teenagers are not likely to view as sufficiently interesting or hip are often disadvantaged in the helping professions' labor market. Professional helpers who do find themselves employed in positions where they must learn to be with edgy youth often misunderstand their role as being akin to becoming an edgy youth and mimic at least some of their cultural characteristics, especially in the context of language use, attire, personal interests and knowledge of current pop or alternative cultures. In fact, this reflects a fundamental misunderstanding about being with edgy youth. In a subtle way, it also expresses a level of disrespect toward edgy youth because it assumes that these young people have a rather limited range of social and personal interests. In fact, edgy youth much prefer to have professional helpers who are unlike their peers, and, at any rate, they are quite competent in their ability to detect fraudulent helpers pretending to be what they are not.

Ultimately, one of the values that is firmly embedded among edgy youth is that of personal strength and self-righteousness. Edgy youth have learned the hard way that the most reliable person in their lives is typically themselves, and it is important to learn to accept oneself and gain strength from one's own identity. Similarly, edgy youth recognize the value of a professional helper who engages them based on his or her identity and sense of self, without making any attempt to adjust to the likes or dislikes of the young person. Strong professional helpers are those who bring themselves to the being with edgy youth, instead of those who mask themselves by seeking to adopt the ways of edgy youth in their engagement of them. Some of the resources that professional helpers bring to being with edgy youth are often taken for granted. It is important that we spell out what these resources are so that professional helpers committed to sticking with edgy youth over time are able to activate these resources as needed. Four such resources quickly come to mind: generational experience, expertise about the center, personal experience of developmental change and coming to terms with hypocrisy. I want to briefly describe each of these below.

Generational Experience – While it is true that the social, political and economic contexts of different generations are indeed different and unique to their times, there are some fundamental characteristics of personal development and growth that change very little with time. Thus, long before the current generation of edgy youth adopted its resistance to the center and to the established ways of doing things, previous generations of young people had experimented with a wide range of approaches to resistance. Furthermore, long before the current generation of edgy youth found comfort in its distance from the center, previous generations had explored the edges of social conformity and compliance. We know enough about change and development to understand that developmental components of growing up co-exist with the ever-changing social ecology of the times and that these developmental components change very little across the generations. Professional helpers are well advised to recognize that their accumulated experiences over time really reflect a generational resource that can be used to good effect in being with edgy youth. They have already experienced the positive and negative effects of resistance, the ways in which resistance is neutralized with the passage of time and the reaching of developmental milestones, and the way in which the spirit of resistance can be preserved even as new, more conforming priorities creep into everyday life.

Expertise about the Center – Edgy youth can significantly benefit from accessing some of the resources available within the center without having to abandon their status as edgy youth and without having to assume a new, more conformist and compliant identity. Knowing how the center works, where to access resources and how to manipulate such resources to serve one's needs is of great importance. Professional helpers are well placed to assist edgy youth in gaining this knowledge and understanding. Indeed, transferring some of the pragmatism required to navigate successfully within the center while maintaining one's personal values and belief systems is one of the core roles that professional helpers can play in the lives of edgy youth. Although part of the rejection of the center is the formality of programs and services found there, even in the center such formality can be transcended through personal connections and relationships. When professional helpers are prepared to share their contacts, connections and professional relationships within the service system with the edgy youth, this can provide opportunities for the youth to create customized and personalized services that meet their specific needs or desires. Even in the context of the center's formality, after all, it matters who one knows; all policy and procedures in the center are subject to overrides by highly placed personnel.

Personal Experiences with Developmental Change – Similar to the opportunities presented through the resource of generational experiences, professional helpers can access their own experiences of developmental growth as a way of guiding young people through theirs. This is an invaluable resource that is often under-utilized as a result of over-zealous approaches to imposing boundaries on helper-youth relationships. The reality is that edgy youth are challenged to distinguish those characteristics of their everyday lives that reflect their status as edgy youth and their need to resist the center on the one hand, and the characteristics that are simply reflective of their developmental change and growth on the other hand. Many of the routine activities and experiences of edgy youth can fall into either category; experimentation with illicit substances, alcohol consumption, sexual activity, laziness, a lack of motivation, depression and a wide range of physiological effects of physical growth can be attributed to pathological trends related to mental health, behavioral disturbances or generalized delinquency, or these can be attributed to perfectly normal developmental milestones. While for most edgy youth it is likely that these kinds of activities and developments reflect developmental milestones within a higher risk of social and personal health contexts than what is typical, there is still a need for professional helpers to assist edgy youth in understanding these changes and developments in context. This is important so that edgy youth do not develop a sense of identity that is based on a view of Self characterized by inevitable deviance and abnormality. While there are many strategies that can be employed in sharing one's own experiences of developmental change and growth, the idea of using those experiences as a resource in being with edgy youth should never be dismissed from the start.

Coming to Terms with Hypocrisy – finally, professional helpers can bring to the experience of being with edgy youth the capacity to come to terms with a generalized hypocrisy that is evident in most aspects of contemporary society. Edgy youth are highly sensitized to hypocrisy in their social surroundings and unfortunately are quick to dismiss all value to messages that are essentially positive and useful, but not always evident in the behavior of the messenger. Examples include: care taking professionals who preach about looking after oneself while at the same time smoking cigarettes, social work professionals who lecture the youth about follow through but then fail to meet their own responsibilities, and messages about problem-solving among peers when it is evident that the professional helpers are unable to resolve problems among themselves. Even at the broader societal level, hypocrisy is evident everywhere and includes messages about environmental protection, from messengers who drive gas-guzzling SUVs, messages about the ills of violence from politicians who promote war abroad, and messages about honesty and integrity from individuals who later turn out to have lived double lives and deceived their families and loved ones. Hypocrisy is all around us and edgy youth often struggle with coming to terms with this. The harsh realities of life on the edge may be troublesome, but edgy youth can take comfort in the integrity and transparency of what happens every day. Professional helpers bring to edgy youth a perspective on living with hypocrisy that reflects a critical view of the perpetrators and also a pragmatic view of how to live in spite of this hypocrisy. As these professional helpers stick with being with edgy youth over time, sharing this enormously important perspective and skill is of great importance.

Much of what I have discussed in this chapter is about recognizing just how much needs to happen in our being with edgy youth in order for them to maintain their spirits and aspirations for the good life. Given the enormity of the task, sticking with it is essential, and being with edgy youth must be recognized not as a time limited task in which all problems are either resolved or the youth are abandoned, but rather as a living social and inter-personal contract that evolves over time to meet head-on the changes that appear for both the youth and the professional helper.

Chapter 6

THE GOOD LIFE ON THE EDGE

One of the greatest misconceptions by professional helpers and their helping systems is that in order for edgy youth to be successful, they must drop their edge. I argue that quite the opposite is true. The edgy youth who will eventually succeed are those who have maintained their edge. The long-term service users and chronic help seekers will be those who gave up their edge and attempted to conform to the commands of their helpers and to comply with the authorities imposed upon them. These edgy youth become soulless youth, youth without dreams, young adults without any fight left in them. Perhaps more importantly, they become young adults without the skills to make it in a world full of contradictions, betrayals, disappointments and dead ends. Indeed, this is not a world that has much to offer to those who simply conform. Nonetheless, it is a world where much is possible for those who tackle it head on, refuse to be brought down, and understand rules to be guidelines, not commands. Making it in this world, especially for young people who may not have glided through their youth with predictable accomplishments in school and a stable status in family and society, requires more than just accepting whatever comes one's way. It requires a mentality that is edgy and skills that speak to the brutality of contemporary social relations.

I want to end this book by highlighting the incredible strengths and competencies that are inherently associated with being an edgy youth. I think it is essential that we come to understand these strengths and competencies because it has been our failure to understand and respect these that has led many edgy youth into a place of despair. Professional helpers, with the best of intentions, have used their training and their commitment to dull the spirit of edgy youth and to condemn the very skills and characteristics that turn out to be essential for survival and for making it in this world. While seeking the best for the young people they work with, many professional helpers and their helping systems have accomplished the worst possible outcome: they have created young adults who no longer believe in where they came from and who don't know where they are going. In this last chapter, I argue that edgy youth ought to be proud of where they came from and they ought to decide for themselves where they want to go. Getting there is not as difficult as it seems; they have already proven their capacity to get to the here and now in spite of enormous adversity. In order to move forward, edgy youth need to reflect on their strengths and competencies that they gained through their developmental journey from child to adolescent to young man or woman. In spite of some of the unfortunate or difficult entanglements they may have experienced or even caused in their lives, there is much to value and nurture in terms of strengths and competencies. I want to highlight ten such strengths and competencies below.

RELATIONSHIPS IN THE MOMENT

Success in contemporary societies is only possible in the context of connections. Knowing people, being connected to individuals and to social groups, feeling a sense of belonging and having a place to be socially engaged are essential characteristics of successfully moving through the days. Yet, the overall culture in North America is moving increasingly in the opposite direction. Here we are promoting a radical brand of individualism where each person is to look after his or her own needs, often in spite of others and sometimes at the expense of others. At every level of society, connections are reinvented to meet the immediate needs of individuals, often in material ways, rather than to form stable and meaningful collectives. Arguably, one of the most critical skills required in contemporary society is that of relationship-making in the moment. Some of the challenges associated with maintaining this skill are the lack of an experiential foundation for such relationships and often minimal authenticity in them. Even concepts such as loyalty, intimacy and commitment are no longer at the core of contemporary relationships; instead, such relationships are about utility, instant gratification and connectivity for mutual benefit.

Edgy youth have spent their entire life building relationships on these very foundations. They have had to find ways of connecting with other edgy youth from all kinds of different walks of life, whether they had things in common or not. They have had to determine an appropriate level of trust for peers and for professional helpers, sometimes in the absence of evidence that such trust will pay off. They have had to take risks, weigh costs and benefits of specific connections, and manage the consequences of connections or relationships that didn't work out. Edgy youth have learned to accept the unpredictable nature of such relationships. Peers and professional helpers may or may not stick around for very long; whatever plans they might make together may or may not be possible to implement. In the end, however, edgy youth have learned to be connected to those available in the moment.

Edgy youth know not only how to form relationships in the moment, but also how to evaluate these on an on-going, even moment-to-moment basis. They know the signs of a deteriorating relationship, of impending trouble as well as of an intensifying or special relationship. Perhaps most importantly, they know about themselves in relationships with others; they learn about their limits and their boundaries, their need for intimacy and for acceptance, but they also learn about managing rejection and relationship breakdowns. Most edgy youth have had more relationship experience, and a more varied relationship experience, than most adults and certainly than most professional helpers. Although they may not have had opportunities to reflect in depth about their relationship history, edgy youth are certainly well placed for the increasingly complex nature of contemporary relationships.

STARTING OVER

Most of us don't deal all that well with abrupt endings, and yet we often face situations where such endings emerge. Whether it is loss of employment, loss of housing, an abrupt termination of a relationship or any other transition that was unexpected and perhaps not wished for, we frequently must make the necessary adjustments to move along our journey of life. This can be very challenging, especially for young people. Most young people thrive under conditions of stability and predictability, and they often become disoriented when things turn out in ways they did not expect. In this respect, edgy youth are not like most young people. Many edgy youth have already had to start over on several occasions. Such starting over could be the result of new placements in group homes, foster homes or extended family, or it could relate to transferring schools, neighborhoods or recreational clubs. Indeed, perhaps most commonly, edgy youth have often had the experience of starting over in relationships, including with respect to entire peer groups, family groups and helping professionals.

Starting over takes considerable skill. As already discussed, the ability to form relationships in the moment is one such skill, but beyond this, edgy youth must be able to draw on their past experiences of starting over and maintain confidence that they can do so again without too much loss or trauma. It takes confidence to enter a new peer group, to become part of a new school environment and certainly to move into a new group home or foster family. It takes considerable focus and observation skills to find one's place among professional helpers and their helping systems. These are the skills that edgy youth have been practicing for much of their lives; thus, starting over is not the end of the world for them. While edgy youth usually do tire from the constant flux in their lives and sometimes may even crave stability and predictability, they certainly have learned to cope in their absence. It helps a great deal to manage oneself in this world when one is able to avoid becoming flustered.

FINDING LOOPHOLES

Yet another challenge these days is to get what one wants in the face of enormous bureaucracies, red tape and institutional policies and procedures that are anything but transparent. Indeed, getting through the complexities of contemporary service systems, whether in the areas of mental health, health care, education, youth justice or professional training and development can be an enormous challenge, even for well-placed adults who have the time to explore the appropriate process and procedures. Still, no matter how patient and sensible one might be, there are times when dead ends appear that seem insurmountable. Even professional helpers whose job it is to facilitate access to programs and services sometimes get stuck in the wilderness of bureaucracy. Edgy youth often have an uncanny ability to circumvent formal processes and procedures, finding the loopholes. Their ability to uncover weakness in bureaucracy, combined with their inhibition related to asking for things, demanding things or simply starting to avail themselves of things serves to quickly get past the formality of process and straight to the heart of the matter. If there is a loophole in a bureaucratic process, edgy youth are usually the most likely to find it.

Perhaps it should not be entirely surprising that edgy youth have this extraordinary skill of finding the loopholes. Much of their own experience has been one of "falling through the cracks", which, by definition, implies that formal processes and procedures that are designed to be inclusive and universally accessible are full of loopholes and exceptions. While they may have experienced the negative aspects of such loopholes in the process of their earlier interactions with institutions and systems, edgy youth wise up to this and begin to turn the table on those very institutions and systems that worked so hard to exclude them by accessing loopholes in their own protocols. In the end, it are those edgy youth who relinquish their edginess who may continue to fall through the cracks; the really edgy ones who recognize the value of their edginess find their way through the labyrinth of formality, one way or another.

MANIPULATION AND PERSUASION

The really good news for edgy youth is that all of the times that they were admonished by their professional helpers for "manipulating" others, the team of helpers or even their peers now turns out to be one of the most useful skills they could have practiced. Manipulation and persuasion are two skills that edgy youth have mastered, likely by necessity given the enormous pressure to comply with the structures and routines offered through the helping systems. The contexts for applying one's manipulation and persuasion skills are virtually endless in contemporary societies and range from getting the best possible deal on housing and the purchase of material things to ensuring access to recreational, professional, and educational opportunities. Indeed, in the absence of having money to offer as a way of getting what one wants, manipulation and persuasion are likely the second best resources to bring to the table.

Throughout their lives, edgy youth have had to manipulate situations and people in order to ensure that their needs and desires were met. Such manipulation is often seen as a negative activity, one that is associated with dishonesty and a lack of transparency. From the perspective of edgy youth, however, manipulation is what they have been subjected to in all kinds of different contexts, including doctors and professional helpers trying to get them to accept pharmacological interventions when these were not needed, peers trying to get them to share toys, money or cigarettes, and families trying to get them to forget their wrong doings and come home. Edgy youth know that manipulation is not so much about lying or wrongfully getting what one wants, but rather is a widely practiced and a nearly universally accepted form of negotiating who gets what, when and how. Similarly, edgy youth know that the power of persuasion is priceless and one that must be honed and fine tuned on an on-going basis. The best way to get things from others is not to impose one's will on them, but to make them believe that giving what one wants is a good idea or at the very least, the right thing to do.[1]

Self-advocacy

Edgy youth are masters at advocating on their own behalf. This is especially true for those edgy youth who refused to conform to the processes and expectations presented to them by their professional helpers. Those who did conform to these expectations often had less opportunity to advocate on their own behalf since much of this was done by the professional helper instead. Edgy youth connected to helping systems typically learn very quickly that the rhetoric about having their voice included in their plans of care, as well as the language of youth empowerment, does not necessarily lead to outcomes they might deem desirable. They have also learned that there are always limits to the extent to which their voices will be heard or even tolerated. Self-advocacy, therefore, is an essential skill that edgy youth need to develop in order to ensure that they matter in the larger scheme of things. Ironically, the very helping systems designed to engage edgy youth often become so preoccupied with their own systemic and organizational issues that the experiences of edgy youth become secondary to the needs of the system or the organizations within it.

Self-advocacy requires a great deal of confidence and personal strength. Not all youth are able to speak up when it matters and express their concerns or desires to groups of adults who typically see themselves as the experts on the young people's needs. Those who do, often do so in a manner that might be seen as indicative of deficits and problems, given the inclusion of profanity and a presentation that may lack some of the nuances of manners and respect. Far from being a deficit, it are these uninhibited interventions on their own behalf that render edgy youth who self-advocate a force to be reckoned with as they grow into adulthood. These are not likely going to be young adults who will easily be put in their place or be made to conform when things appear not quite right or unjust.

---

[1] This is essentially Gramsci's notion of the hegemony in which the dominant forces are maintaining a broad culture of support for their dominance, and those being oppressed believe this culture speaks to their needs (Gramsci, 2007).

LANGUAGE SKILLS AND PROFESSIONAL EXPOSURE

Anyone who has spent time with edgy youth embedded in the helping systems might be surprised to find out that these young people often have enormously sophisticated language skills and an understanding of the professional world that far exceeds that of most young people. While engaging edgy youth in groups often results in the lowest representation of language and a mannerism that seems primitive and vulgar, on a one-on one basis, these same young people can very often provide articulate, critical and well thought out descriptions and analyses of the service system, the professional helpers they have encountered and of the socio-political context in which services are provided. It is not uncommon, in fact, for edgy youth to be able to articulate the nuances of the helping professions and helping systems in a more sophisticated manner than the professional helpers.

This should not be completely surprising. After all, edgy youth often experience greater exposure to the professional world of the helping system and to the language associated with this world than most young people, and sometimes even more than individual professional helpers. Whereas such professional helpers often find themselves quite isolated in their specific tasks and roles, the edgy youth move through a wide range of service settings each day where they encounter different aspects of the system. They might live in a residential facility, attend a special education school, receive counseling in a mental health clinic and occasionally spend some time in custody. As such, these young people become intimately familiar not only with how different elements of the system work, but also with the respective language spoken and how that language either promotes or inhibits certain actions or decisions. Edgy youth graduate from the helping systems having had an intensive and in depth exposure to professional language and work, and having gained an understanding of team work, professional conflict, organizational change, hierarchy, and many other professional processes.

THE VALUE OF STORIES

Adversity sells. This may seem like an odd statement, but the reality is that contemporary society thrives on the stories of adversity faced by other people. Indeed, hearing a young person relate their story of adversity is usually seen as inspiring, even if that young person has yet to overcome his or her adversity. Most young people have not much of a story to tell. Their experiences are unique and special to them, but when articulated for broader consumption, these stories appear a little dull and unremarkable. The stories of edgy youth, in contrast, are never dull and they certainly are remarkable in the sense that they often are replete with situations that are difficult to even imagine. The stories about trauma and abuse, abandonment and rejection invoke empathy for the young people because they are not seen to be at fault for these experiences. More remarkable, however, is that other sorts of stories also invoke empathy and sometimes even admiration. This includes stories about substance use, sexual activity, violence and gang activities as well as other criminal activities. Somehow, just telling the stories appears to be an experience for those listening, and often is enough to invoke a preparedness on the part of others (adults, employers, funders) to provide assistance to the young people who tell these stories. As edgy youth approach young adulthood, they are not only edgy youth, but also interesting youth, and this generates a value that can be harvested.

ENTREPRENEURSHIP

For most edgy youth, the recommended path to adulthood is one that is all too familiar to most of us. Finish high school and consider a trade or any sort of gainful employment in order to get started on life as an independent adult. Indeed, most helping systems provide programs and services for edgy youth about to age-out of youth services that specifically seek to help these youth get as far down this path as possible. Such programs are often referred to as pre-independence training, semi-independence programs or preparation courses for independent living (Berzin & Taylor, 2009; Naccarato & DeLorenzo, 2008). The goal of these programs is to get young people started on the road to conformity, where life is about working and paying one's dues. Not surprisingly, many edgy youth don't get very far with this approach and either fail to complete their pre-independence training or, once they become independent, simply stop following what they learned during the training. The reality is that edgy youth are not very good at working for others, at following the often very firm structure and expectations of the work place and at maintaining a longer term view of the benefits of work and a steady income. Instead, most look for instant gratification for some level of control over their everyday activities, and much greater levels of excitement and risk in their work life.

If we think about where such characteristics tend to be desirable, we might quickly notice that these are the core characteristics of the entrepreneurial spirit. Indeed, the desire to be in charge of oneself, to take risks, to manage the unpredictable and to make it on one's own are all core elements of being an entrepreneur. Edgy youth are well qualified to pursue entrepreneurial careers and initiatives, given their experience of risk and risk management in everyday life. Indeed, one might argue that edgy youth have opportunities here that could place them at the helm of the youth initiative movement and provide the framework for leadership for young people everywhere. What is often characterized as a shortcoming of edgy youth can easily be reframed as a major strength. The inability of edgy youth to find satisfaction in the conformity required to pursue menial work in minimum wage industries, such as the fast food industry or general labor, is a real strength that complements some of the other strengths identified above. It does seem that a young person with excellent persuasive skills, the ability to start over easily, a capacity for in the moment relationship development and an extensive exposure to professional language and conduct would be particularly well placed to pursue entrepreneurial initiatives.

GROUP DYNAMICS

Almost nothing happens in this world without there being a group of initiators, collaborators or supporters who direct what happens next. Indeed, although there has been a major entrenchment of individualism in many Western societies, in particular, at the level of community or business activity, virtually everything is driven by groups of people rather than by individuals. Within most initiatives, participants are interdependent. Therefore, it is extremely important that young people entering the world of adults and professional activity are well versed in the complexities of group dynamics.

Again, we can identify this as a real strength on the part of edgy youth. Many edgy youth have literally grown up in group contexts, particularly if they have spent substantial periods of time in residential group care. They have had to learn about the group process, collective responsibility, group problem-solving as well as how to occupy leadership positions within groups and the implications of being marginalized within these. Their experience extends beyond managing themselves in peer groups, and also includes experience in observing and managing groups of professionals seeking to have input into their plans of care or intervention strategies. Indeed, edgy youth understand groups better than most people, and they certainly have found strategies to be noticed in groups and to have an impact on groups of people. Once again, we can see the connection between this strength and some of the other strengths already identified above. The ability of edgy youth to form relationships in the moment is a great asset in relation to managing group dynamics. In this way, the youth can form alliances, connections and partnerships, both within existing groups as well as in their efforts to enter new groups.

Edgy youth are not easily intimidated. Even very imposing group dynamics are recognized as opportunities to position oneself as a potential leader, and edgy youth are typically sufficiently confident about their identity and capacities to make their presence known to all members of such groups.

RECOVERY FROM LOSS

Finally, I want to cite one other strength deeply embedded in the life experiences of edgy youth. This is the capacity to recover very quickly from major personal loss. This is a significant strength that cannot be underestimated. Many young people spend significant periods of time being a victim and presenting as such to others. Whatever loss they may have suffered, be it related to losing a loved one who has died or simply becoming alienated from family or peer groups, this kind of loss takes a great deal of time to recover from for many youth. During this time, many opportunities for starting over are missed, and some of the other strengths that are discussed above are deactivated. Edgy youth, on the other hand, have already experienced a great deal of loss and have typically learned that loss can be grieved as part of the recovery process; there is no need to wait for the grieving process to be complete before recovery begins.

Edgy youth are enormously resilient in the face of repeated loss. They often have lost members of their family; placements; neighborhoods, communities, important peer groups, or individual peers. Still, these youth continue to reinvent themselves, to make new connections, start new relationships, and continue to look forward and work towards a future. Although recovery from loss should not be seen as an indication of having resolved one's grief, it allows edgy youth to continue to move forward and apply all of the strengths and competencies already discussed. Ups and downs are to be expected in the journey to adulthood and independence, and having a capacity to recover quickly from losses in order to maintain the momentum forward is, without a doubt, useful.

These are ten areas of strength and competency held by edgy youth that are often not acknowledged, either by professional helpers or by society at large. The behavior of edgy youth, including their apparent preference for obscene language and poor social manners, often present an image of absolute vulnerability and societal burden. Media reports about the latest crimes, vandalism, and the poor social and economic performance of edgy youth have contributed to a societal view of them as problematic and in need of either intervention or social marginalization. In fact, edgy youth have much to offer to our society. Their experiences of living life on the edge are very compatible with what is needed in contemporary societies to exercise leadership and to engage critically with some of the features of our societies that seem outdated, destructive or simply unsustainable. We can think of, for example, the environmental challenges facing the planet and the need to address these challenges in a bold and sweeping manner. Clearly, this will not happen under the leadership of young people who have been trained to conform to the commands of the power centers of this world. Those young people are most likely to maintain the status quo, either intentionally or inadvertently, sometimes being aware of their subservience and at other times believing themselves to be activists when they are simply reinforcing the power structures already in place. Edgy youth are our most valuable resource in ensuring that someone will challenge what is happening with the environment and with the other global pressures on humanity that are currently being largely ignored.

The reality is, however, that many edgy youth experience a disempowerment and dismissal to such an extent, in their association with professional helpers and their helping systems, that they lose their edge altogether by the time they reach adulthood. After years of interventions, treatment and care plans developed by adults and reflecting the values of conformity and compliance, these edgy youth no longer believe in themselves. They enter the next stages of their lives without anything to hold to. Their identities are weakened, their resolve to move forward is wobbly and their capacity to recover from failure or loss is minimal. They have been taught to rely on their professional helpers to resolve problems and challenges, or, at the very least, they have learned that whenever they might fail to meet expectations that consequences will be imposed to remind them of the proper path. Unfortunately, this means that when they are left to their own devices, they become indecisive, insecure and overwhelmed by all that needs to be considered and all that needs to be done. Throughout this book, I have argued that we must rescue edgy youth from our attempts to take their edge away. The best way, indeed the only way, to do this is to learn to be with edgy youth. Being, as I argued in earlier chapters, is not a passive exercise with no substantive content, but rather a skill-based and even artful way of engaging young people whose lives are fundamentally different than ours. Their commitment to the edge is strong and so our commitment to respecting theirs is vital. Below, I want to sketch out four important strategies of being with edgy youth, adding to some of the other approaches, strategies and considerations already developed throughout this book. These four strategies of being with edgy youth very explicitly draw on the strengths and competencies of edgy youth described above.

RELATIONSHIP REFLECTIONS

Few people have more interesting stories to tell about relationships than edgy youth. Most edgy youth can tell stories about relationships that range from abusive and violent to those that are nurturing and restorative. Their relationships include those with family members, professionals, peers and people they meet in passing as they pass through many different settings and places. Edgy youth are good at forming relationships and making connections with others; they have had to become good at this because the only way to connect to the latest version of their life (manifested by yet another placement change, more professionals involving themselves in their care or treatment or more exposure to school programs and community services), is to find connections to the people around them, even if such connections sometimes turn out to be very short term.

The constant need to connect with others and to have relationships with individuals and groups of people who may or may not have much in common with oneself is difficult and confusing. The reason for relationship is not based on a mutual liking or some common purpose; instead, the reasons for the relationship are varied and often impossible to identify with any clarity. Nevertheless, the skill involved in developing relationships and making connections is noteworthy. Most edgy youth are not in a position to really take note of this skill and reflect on where and how they might apply this skill in a more strategic and meaningful manner.

Professional helpers can integrate a focus of reflecting on relationships into their everyday being with edgy youth. Indeed, I would argue that this is one of the most important contributions professional helpers can make to the lives of edgy youth. Helping the young person reflect on their past and current relationships, and exploring why some relationships seem to produce experiences that are worthwhile and desirable while others seem to produce only negativity and problems, is an invaluable service. Edgy youth who contemplate their past and present relationships are able to formulate plans for their relationship future. Young people who allow relationships to unfold in the absence of any reflection or contemplation often take for granted both the benefits and the drawbacks of relationships. Consequently, they never really move beyond the observer status in their own relationships.

For these reasons, professional helpers ought to be interested in the relationship past of the edgy youth that they are engaging. Such interest must extend beyond the obvious familial relationships of mother and father and also include siblings and extended family as well as significant others in their social circles. Particularly important in this context is paying attention to how edgy youth determine the degree of importance associated with the various kinds of relationships in their lives. Understanding how importance in this context is allocated will assist edgy youth in understanding their own biases and preconceived notions in terms of their social connections and personal relationships.

Reflecting on their past and present relationships is not only a critical process for the purpose of understanding future relationships, but also for the purpose of gaining confidence that the pursuit of relationships is a worthwhile endeavor in and of itself, and that it is possible to determine the direction of relationship even if one's experiences in relationships have often been very negative. In this sense, being with edgy youth is fundamentally about constructing a relationship history that is very unique to the particular young person that the professional helper is engaging, and that is owned by the young person in its entirety. In so doing, the professional helper will not only assist the young person in building a strong foundation for future relationships, but also in reflectively developing the relationship between helper and young person in the here and now. Thus, being with edgy youth becomes an inherently relational process.

NURTURING THE ENTREPRENEURIAL SPIRIT

Above, I briefly discussed the manner in which the more combative elements within the character of many edgy youth can constitute a real strength from an entrepreneurial point of view. Entrepreneurship is a potential pathway for edgy youth to maintain their identity and their resistance toward conformity, while still creating opportunities for material growth and development. Indeed, helping edgy youth capitalize on their entrepreneurial spirit ought to be one of the priorities of professional helpers seeking to engage these young people. In most service settings, however, edgy youth are discouraged from pursuing entrepreneurial activities and instead are encouraged to pursue the very things that they have previously failed to accomplish. Whether it is school completion, formal apprenticeship programs or simply following through each and every day with attending to a minimum wage job in a dead end industry, professional helpers and their helping systems often, and inadvertently, have pushed edgy youth to abandon any pretense at pursuing economic activity that might pay for their autonomy.

Instead, professional helpers engaging edgy youth ought to assist these young people in developing their entrepreneurial skills further and in experimenting with entrepreneurial activities in areas of interest to the young persons. In being with edgy youth, professional helpers can take note of the entrepreneurial skills and talents of particular young people and ensure that these are discussed and reflected upon with them. At a more practical level, being with edgy youth can also involve exposing the youth to opportunities for grants and other contributions to youth-driven entrepreneurial initiatives that are widely available in most societies. Interestingly, virtually none of the pre-independence training programs for edgy youth contain any information about entrepreneurship, starting one's own business or government or foundation grant programs for young people to pursue their entrepreneurial dreams. It is time for those professional helpers engaged with edgy youth to develop and strengthen the young people's entrepreneurial talents and then to risk along with them some actual entrepreneurial initiatives.

MANAGE TRAUMA

One of the mistakes often made by professional helpers when being with edgy youth is to misinterpret their progress toward material autonomy an indicator of a past trauma's resolution. In fact, nothing could be further from the truth. It is essential that professional helpers recognize that the trauma that was already experienced by the edgy youth is not a "resolvable trauma" and that the implications of this trauma are always at risk of resurfacing or of re-manifesting themselves in different ways. As much as edgy youth have enormous strength and resilience in terms of the adversities faced during their lives on the edge, they also maintain the vulnerabilities that resulted in their earlier victimization or marginalization, and, in many cases, additional trauma builds alongside successes and positive developments as the youth moves into adulthood.

Therefore, professional helpers must always focus their being with edgy youth on managing whatever trauma might be surfacing at any given time. Exploring the roots of trauma and developing strategies to manage such trauma are essential activities in the helper-youth relationship. Specifically, as one of their functions, professional helpers must fulfill the task of reminding edgy youth that trauma continues to be present in their lives and that this cannot simply be wished away. Although this may not be a positive message that promotes inspiration and might motivate the young person to perform well in whatever his or her current endeavor might be, it is a far better message than allowing the young person to be surprised or overwhelmed by the sudden reappearance of trauma when it was least expected.

REMEMBERING THE PAST AND BUILDING THE FUTURE

Professional helpers and even society at large sometimes underestimate the challenges associated with building a future that is fundamentally disconnected from one's past. Yet, this is precisely what we often do when we ask edgy youth to abandon their edge and to conform to the standards and expectations presented by the helping systems and various stakeholders in the community. In this book, I have argued that edgy youth weaken the foundation for their future when they agree to abandon their past on the edge. Contrary to commonly expressed perspectives, there is a great deal of strength and competency associated with life on the edge, and professional helpers need to find ways of being with edgy youth that help them to connect the past and the future through a presence that acknowledges both strengths and challenges related to their unique circumstances. This is also one of the reasons why it is important for professional helpers to learn to be with edgy youth; it is only through being with edgy youth that they can begin to understand the unique nature of each young person's life and experiences. Being an edgy youth does not result in being the same as every other edgy youth. Given the uniqueness of each young person's edginess, it is imperative that professional helpers employ unique approaches to connecting the past to the future. Remembering the past along with the edgy youth requires an attention to the details of the past, and these details ought to have an impact on the specific features of the future that is being built.

"BEING WITH" AS THE INTERVENTION

My argument throughout this book has been that being with edgy youth is the intervention. This is a bold argument because it marginalizes more traditional forms of intervention such as treatment, behavior therapy, or other change-oriented approaches. In doing so, I am not suggesting that change is unnecessary. Lest anyone accuse me of naïveté or simply of failing to take reality into account, I want to be clear that I fully recognize the risks and safety concerns faced by edgy youth every day. I am aware that many live their lives in misery and pain, and some will die as a result of violence, suicide or preventable illness. I also acknowledge the risks and safety concerns faced by neighborhoods and communities where edgy youth live. Although the association of crime with young people is much exaggerated, it is understandable that people in otherwise quiet neighborhoods experience unease and concern about the presence and often challenging conduct of edgy youth in their midst. Some edgy youth commit crimes, many consume drugs and alcohol and most are associated with violence from time to time, even if most of the time they are the victims of violence, rather than the initiators. It is fair to conclude that our thinking about edgy youth is serious business, and whatever perspective we adopt will have its worth measured against the violence, death and destruction that edgy youth both perpetrate and experience.

Nonetheless, I still maintain that we need to back off our enthusiastic endorsements of the latest fads in the treatment of young people affected by mental health challenges, behavioral problems or a generalized instability and lack of conformity. As much as evidence-based practices provide for confidence among professional helping systems that their efforts will be rewarded with positive outcomes for their clients, we must acknowledge that no matter how positive the outcome, these will never capture everybody. In every service, program, and initiative designed to address the challenges facing young people there will be those who benefit and those who don't. It is the group of young people who chronically fail to benefit from traditional interventions, seeming to always end up on the outside looking in, that we need to focus on. It is with respect to this group of young people that we must acknowledge our catastrophic failure. We have accomplished nothing for these young people other than driving them further to the edge of the edge, and, in some cases, providing all but the final push over the edge.

There is an ethical element in my argument. I would suggest that as a society and certainly as a helping system, we reach the limits of ethical conduct when we continuously offer services to edgy youth that we can safely predict will fail. Our ethics become rather fragile when we become complacent with respect to the prognoses for those edgy youth who are non-conforming and non-compliant with our expectations. Furthermore, we most certainly abandon all pretense of ethical behavior when we eventually abandon our edgy youth because they just would not listen, rationalizing this abandonment by blaming the youth. We must do better than this. We must learn to be with edgy youth in a way that they, too, wish to be with us. We must learn to transcend the logistical limitations of employment schedules and program structures to expand our being with edgy youth into all aspects of their life space, including the physical, virtual, relational and mental dimensions of their life space.

Being with edgy youth means that we must take the everyday moments of their existence seriously. It means that we must be interested in their mundane experiences of life as much as in their more extraordinary experiences, relationships and situations. Ultimately, being with edgy youth means that we are present in their journey through adolescence and into adulthood, sharing the hardships and the successes along the way. We are not passive observers of this journey. To our joined journey, we bring wisdom and honest feedback, information and emotional responses to the actions and decisions of the youth. We are there every step of the way, sometimes in ways that will make the youth smile, and often in ways that will make them cringe, but we are there. We avoid the trappings of treatment and predetermined directions for change because we know that the youth have already tried all of these to the best of their abilities. They have made attempts at conformity and compliance before, and they have learned, for better or for worse, that this will not work for them. Edgy youth are neither broken nor sick. Therefore, they do not need us to fix them or heal them. Instead, they need us to be with them.

Being with edgy youth is not just a different way of behaving as a professional helper or a different way of designing professional helping systems. It is much more than that. To end this book, I want to present my final argument as this: being with edgy youth is a commitment to democracy in the helping professions, and it is also a pragmatic approach to ensure that our societies can rely on radical, innovative, confident and pragmatic leaders and leadership in the future.

THE COMMITMENT TO DEMOCRACY

A democratic approach to being with edgy youth does not call for empowerment as much as it calls for a deep respect for self-determination. The distinction between these two concepts is a significant one. This distinction reflects some of the differences between a benevolent autocracy and real democracy. The former system works hard to benefit the edgy youth based on the values and beliefs of those holding power within that system. The intentions are good, but the process is fundamentally undemocratic and largely controlled by very few people professing to be experts and the holders of truth. The knowledge base for interventions is difficult to access for those who will be impacted by such interventions, and even when it can be accessed, it is based on concepts and language that is unfamiliar, technical and rooted in perspectives of the everyday experiences of edgy youth that they are out of touch with. Within such benevolent autocracies, there is room to allow for voice on the part of the young people and perhaps even their supporters, but the decision-making system is ultimately extremely hierarchical, with the "super-experts" (often psychiatrists) at the top of the pyramid. The goal of intervention is never really questioned; it is to transform the edgy youth into a compliant young person who performs at adequate levels within the institutions and systems of mainstream society.

Autocracy is difficult to critique. The positive intentions that can be easily articulated in accordance with dominant social values are often backed up by evidence of positive outcomes. Many young people who appeared to be struggling in school or at home can be shown to experience fewer struggles following an autocratic intervention. As such, autocracy is perpetually reinforced as an entirely reasonable and successful system of intervention, and the few individuals at the helm of autocratic intervention continue to be celebrated as the ultimate experts on youth issues, ranging from developmental growth to psychopathology.[2]

---

[2] This dynamic is clearly observable in the manner in which packaged and trademarked approaches to intervention have their clinical merits evolve in tandem with their marketing

Aside from outcomes, autocratic systems have other benefits as well. For one thing, they allow those at the center of the process to control the costs of interventions. By elevating the scientific foundation of the intervention as its core element instead of recognizing the intervener as the agent of change, those engaged with young people every day in whatever settings the young people are to be found can be marginalized and systematically under-valued. Even the voice of young people can be marginalized since it has no basis in scientific foundations. Ultimately, the extent to which young people are given a voice at all is not really related to the outcomes of the intervention. Instead, it is simply a measure of well-meaning and good intentions on the part of the experts at the top of the intervention process.

None of this is compatible with a democratic approach to intervention. Democracy requires much more than the appearance of good intentions and processes that produce outcomes deemed positive when based on an *a priori* defined set of values. Democracy requires partnerships and collaborative processes that involve all of the stakeholders in tangible and concrete ways, allowing for decision-making processes that are neither hierarchical nor entirely consensual. Instead, within a democratic approach to intervention, all of the stakeholders spend considerable time getting to know each others' expertise, and there is clarity from the start that expertise is not exclusive to the realm of science. Quite to the contrary, given the focus on the everyday experiences of young people, expertise is constituted much more so by how young people experience the mundane and the extraordinary and how they make sense of these experiences, rather than by an externally derived, systematic approach to change. At the same time, democracy does not require the blind acceptance and celebration of whatever it is edgy youth desire or deem appropriate. Professional helpers are also empowered to express their points of view and to challenge young people on core issues and themes. Professional helpers do not have to support decisions made by young people if these do not correspond with their own beliefs or values, or if they believe such decisions are likely to produce negative outcomes. What differentiates a democratic approach from the autocratic approach, however, is that the ownership over what happens next is shared at all times, and neither professional helper nor their helping systems are in a position to enforce their priorities over those of the young person.

---

success. In the 1990s, the rise of 1, 2, 3 Magic as the fool proof response to child and youth behavioral problems seemed to resolve the issues for good (Phelan, 1995); currently, we have a similar magic bullet in the form of collaborative problem solving, first introduced by Ross Greene (2010).

Democratic approaches to intervention recognize the chronic presence of risk and threats to the safety and well-being of the young person and possibly of his or her social context as well. Professional helpers maintain their obligation, legal and ethical, to mitigate such risks and to ensure that prevention measures are in place to keep the young people safe. Such measures, however, are not control-based measures such as forcible containment, threat of consequences or withholding the access to certain people or places. Instead, the specific measures taken to ensure the safety and well-being of the young person are all subsumed in being with the young person. Being with the young person is, therefore, not only a reactive intervention, but also a prevention strategy. By being with the young person, professional helpers are able to anticipate safety concerns and work in partnership with the young person to develop strategies to mitigate these concerns. Being with edgy youth, in particular, avoids the emergence of sudden crises that then require autocratic responses for the sake of safety. Being with edgy youth provides opportunities to anticipate impending problems in advance and to work jointly toward meaningful approaches to resolving such problems or to accepting their consequences.

Democratic approaches to intervention are an essential element of being with edgy youth. This is the case as edgy youth have all too often had negative experiences with the good intentions of autocratic approaches to intervention, even when these are offered within those organizational frameworks that are specifically designed to benefit the young people. Such frameworks might include child welfare systems, children's mental health programs or even services for children and youth living at home in struggling families; edgy youth have earned the title "edgy" specifically because of their rejection of what is being offered by the helping professionals and their helping systems. Edgy youth are not prepared to be reduced to recipients of assistance; they want to be the agents of change in their own lives, and they are looking for professional helpers prepared to join their journey, rather than those insisting on their abandoning their journey and joining the conformist majority. It is because of this that I will end this book with the argument that we all have a vested interest to move toward democratization in our approaches to being with edgy youth. The leadership within our societies requires what edgy youth have to offer. We must begin to look past the problems and recognize the enormous potential that these youth have to lead us to a better place.

THE FUTURE IS EDGY

We are rapidly approaching a time of serious crisis in the history of humanity on this planet. Environmentally, we are threatened by what we have done to the air that we breathe, by the scarcity of fresh water, by insufficient energy supplies that are sustainable and renewable, and even by what will soon be an insufficient food supply to feed the planet's 7 billion people. Economically, we are threatened by the enormous debt loads of Western countries, an ever increasing unemployment rate as well as unsustainable costs in pensions, welfare and health care. Globalization is challenging our sense of belonging, our acceptance of diversity and our ability to manage local priorities in the face of global opportunities. The margins between rich and poor all over the world, including in the richest countries of the world, are expanding. Wars and violence continue unabated and the world is facing the real or imagined threat of international terrorism. Perhaps most disturbingly, our political leadership is bankrupt, hopelessly mired in endless name calling, propaganda production, ideological nonsense, patronage, behind the scenes deals and alliances of convenience. Never before have Western democracies experienced the level of political incompetence they are witnessing now. Even with the election of Obama in the United States on a platform of political reform to bring democracy back to the people, nothing is changing for the better. Our leadership has run out of steam, lacks creativity and is very quickly moving all of us toward some really bad times.

Given these bleak developments and the dire need for better leadership, what sorts of characteristics will we need in the next generation of leaders? Who will be there to shake things up? It is not easy to answer this sweeping question, but it is relatively straight forward to figure out whom we don't want to be in charge anymore. We cannot afford the bureaucrats who do little more than cheer on the politicians; we certainly cannot afford the politicians who lack the courage to take initiative. We don't want religious fanatics of any faith to lead us anywhere; we have seen the outcomes of that approach. Finally, we don't want moral grandstanders, the people who tell us what is right and wrong, who gets privileges and who does not, and who is celebrated and who must be marginalized to lead us into the next phase of our collective future.

Although what we don't want and really cannot afford with respect to our leadership is fairly clear, it seems that we are taking no action at all to prevent these kinds of people from once again taking on leadership roles. In all of our institutions and organizations, we continue to promote blind conformity and uncritical compliance. We send our children to schools that have not produced a radical thought in decades and that take virtually all of their instructions from the very bureaucracies that have nearly destroyed the planet and all living things. In the context of interventions for young people who seem to not conform to our expectations, we have clearly committed to deadening their difference. Everything we do is geared toward recreating more of the same; individuals who will accept what is and do nothing to change the insanity of contemporary politics, economics or environmental neglect.

I want to argue that we need edgy youth more now than ever before. We need these young people to aspire to leading us out of the mess we have created. We need leaders who can bridge the past and the future without compromising what they stand for and without giving an inch to anyone who wants to change, own or control them. We need defenders of justice and everyone's right to assume whatever identity fits for them. We need edgy youth to remind us that when the center collapses all that we will have left is the edge; and who knows that edge better than edgy youth?

I believe very strongly that we must maintain at least a small cadre of edgy youth and learn to be with them. I reject the idea that we treat edgy youth for as long as we can, but we abandon them if they prove to be untreatable. If we do this, we should not expect their assistance when we run out of room to mess up our planet. We have much to learn from edgy youth and much to gain from their success within their edginess, rather than their struggles in abandoning their edginess and conforming to the dysfunction of the majority.

In the end, we need leadership that is comfortable in the chaos of democracy; leadership that can navigate instability and uncertain futures without resorting to autocracy or authoritarianism. We need leaders who, when challenged to serve the rich, the privileged and the powerful, can respond in the way that they have always responded to cowardly threats. When everything is at stake and our future hangs in the balance, we need edgy youth to say, "f@ck you".

REFERENCES

Anglin, J. (2002). This month – what people are doing. *CYC-Online*, Issue 38 (March), retrieved on August 29, 2007 from www.cyc-net.org/cyc-online/cycol-0302-anglin.html

Bays, E. (2009). *Indian residential schools: Another picture*. Ottawa: Baico Publishers.

Bazemore, G.S. & Schiff, M. (2005). *Juvenile justice reform and restorative justice: Building theory and policy from practice*. Portland, OR: Willan.

Beautrais, A.L. (2003). Suicide and serious suicide attempts in youth: A multi-group comparison study. *The American Journal of Psychiatry*, (160), 1093-1099.

Berscheid, E. (1999). The greening of relationship science. *American Psychologist*, 54 (4), 260-266.

Berzin, S.C. & Taylor, S.A. (2009). Preparing foster youth for independent living: Collaboration between county independent living programs and community-based youth serving agencies. *Journal of Public Child Welfare*, 3 (3), 254-274.

Cearley, S. (2004). The power of supervision in child welfare services. *Child and Youth Care Forum*, 33 (5), 313-327.

Crosbie-Burnett, M. & Giles-Sims, J. (1994). Adolescent adjustment and step parenting styles. *Family Relations*, 43 (4), 394-399.

Cullen, D. (2009). *Columbine*. New York: Twelve.

Dickason, O.P. & McNab, D.T. (2002). Canada's First Nations: A history of founding peoples from earliest times. Oxford, UK: Oxford University Press.

Flynn, R., Marquis, R., Paquet, M. & Peeke, L. (2011). *Effects of tutoring by foster parents on foster children's academic skills in reading and math: A randomized effectiveness trial*. Ottawa, ON: Center for Research on Educational and Community Services.

Finlay, J. (2005). The use of power and control by incarcerated youth. *Relational Child and Youth Care Practice*, 18 (4), 33-47.

Garfat, T. (Ed.) (2003). *A child and youth care approach to working with families*. New York: Haworth Press.

Garfat, T. (2008). The inter-personal in-between: An exploration of relational child and youth care practice. In G. Bellefuille & F. Ricks (Eds.), *Standing on the precipice: Inquiry into the creative potential of child and youth care practice* (pp. 7-34). Edmonton, AB: McEwan Press.

Gharabaghi, K. (2009). The (potential) ultra-conservatism of resilience theory. *CYC OnLine*, 125 (July), retrieved from http://www.cyc-net.org/cyc-online/cyconline-july2009-gharabaghi.html

Gharabaghi, K. (2010). Three profoundly stupid ideas. *CYC OnLine*, 138 (August), retrieved from http://www.cyc-net.org/cyc-online/cyconline-aug2010-gharabaghi.html

Gharabaghi, K. & Phelan, J. (2011). Beyond control: Staff perceptions of accountability for children and youth in residential group care. *Residential Treatment for Children & Youth*, 28 (1), 75-90.

Gharabaghi, K. & Stuart, C. (2012). *Right here, right now: Exploring life space intervention with children and youth*. Toronto: Pearson Press.

Gramsci, A. (2007). *The prison notebook*. New York: Columbia University Press.

Greene, R. (2010). *The explosive child: A new approach for understanding and parenting easily frustrated, "chronically inflexible" children (Revised 4th edition)*. New York: Harper Collins.

Hayden, C. & Gough, D. (2010). *Implementing restorative justice in children's residential care*. Portland, OR: Policy Press.

Internations" Justice Federation, (nd). *The unknown orphan memorial*. Retrieved on August 25, 2011 from http://www.restoringdignity.org/orphan2.html

Krueger, M. (2004). Personal sources of satisfaction. *CYC-Online*, Issue 68 (September), retrieved on September 17, 2007 from www.cyc-net.org/cyc-online/cycol-0904-satisfaction.html

Kutash, K., Duchnowski, A.J., Lynn, A. (2006). *School-based mental health: An empirical guide for decision-makers*. Tampa, Fl: University of South Florida, The Luis de la Parte Florida Mental Health Institute, Department of Child and Mental Health Studies, Research and Training Center for Children's Mental Health.

Kunzler, J.H. (1993). *The geography of nowhere: The rise and decline of America's man-made landscape*. New York: Simon & Schuster.

Liebenberg, L. & Ungar. M. (Eds.) (2008). Resilience in action: Working with youth across cultures and contexts. Toronto: University of Toronto Press.

Magnuson, D. & Burger, L. (2001). Developmental supervision in residential care. *Journal of Child and Youth Care*, 15 (1), 9-22.

Martin, W. (2009). Stepmonster: A new look at why real stepmothers think, feel and act the way they do. Boston: Houghton, Mifflin, Harcourt.

Naccarato,T. & DeLorenzo, E. (2008). Transitional youth services: Practice implications from a systematic review. *Child and Adolescent Social Work Journal*, 25 (4), 287-308.

Nightingale, E. (2000). Qualities of a child and youth care worker. *CYC-Online*, Number 16 (May), retrieved on August 29, 2007 from www.cyc-net.org/cyc-online/cycol-0500-editor.html

Phelan, T. (1995). *1,2,3 Magic: Effective discipline for children, 2-12*. Glen Ellyn, IL: Parentmagic.

Sadeler, C. & Gharabaghi, K. (2007). What's wrong with them? Youth, the culture of fear and kids on the edge. *Child and Family Journal*, 10 (2), 5-12.

Salhani, D. & Charles, G. (2007). The dynamics of an inter-professional team: The interplay of child and youth care of other professions within a residential treatment milieu. *Relational Child and Youth Care Practice*, 20 (4), 12-20.

Stuart, C. (2008). Shaping the rules: Child and youth care boundaries in the context of relationships. Bonsai! In G. Bellefuille & F. Ricks (Eds.), *Standing on the precipice: Inquiry into the creative potential of child and youth care practice* (pp. 135-168). Edmonton, AB: McEwan Press.

Stuart, C. (2007). Values, habits and relationships. *Relational Journal of Child and Youth Care Practice*, 20 (1), 4-5.

Stuart, C. & Gharabaghi, K. (2010). *Personalized services delivery for young people and families: A synthesis review*. Retrieved from http://digitalcommons.ryerson.ca/cyc/3/

Szalavitz, M. (2006). *Help at any cost: How the troubled-teen industry cons parents and hurts kids*. New York: Penguin Group.

Ungar, M. (Ed.) (2005). *Handbook for working with children and youth: Pathways to resilience across cultures and contexts*. Thousand Oaks: SAGE Publications.

INDEX

DATE DUE	RETURNED